Alexander Hamilton's Famous Report on Manufactures

Made to Congress December 5, 1791, in His Capacity as Secretary of the Treasury

Alexander Hamilton

SOTHIS PRESS

ISBN 978-1-0365-1895-0

This edition is published by
Sothis Press © 2023. The company
is registered in England and Wales.
The Company Number is 14900389.

ALEXANDER HAMILTON'S

FAMOUS

Report on Manufactures

Made to Congress December 5, 1791,

IN HIS CAPACITY AS

SECRETARY OF THE TREASURY.

BOSTON, 1892:
PUBLISHED BY THE HOME MARKET CLUB.
Price, Postpaid, 20 Cents.

POTTER PUBLISHING CO., BOSTON.

U. S. Treasury dept.

ALEXANDER HAMILTON'S

FAMOUS

Report on Manufactures

MADE TO CONGRESS

December 5, 1791,

In His Capacity as Secretary of the Treasury.

INTRODUCTION.

As ALEXANDER HAMILTON is generally recognized as the father of the protective system in America, it is well for all students of this branch of political economy to go to the fountain-head. His famous Report on Manufactures has long been out of print, except in the volumes of his works. To meet a popular demand, this more convenient pamphlet is issued.

Much of the fore part is devoted to arguments against the widely prevalent theory of his time that manufactures were harmful to society, and that a purely agricultural country would be happiest and best. This has no bearing to-day, but is of interest, as showing how, even then, foreign influence had worked for the advantage of European manufacturers upon the American mind.

The latter part abounds in points almost equally pertinent to-day, and sheds light upon the conditions of manufactures and of ocean freights which shows that the nominally low *ad valorem* rates of the earlier tariffs were relatively higher and more protective than the increased duties of the present.

The portrait is from a picture by Trumbull, painted in 1792 for Mr. George Cabot. This portrait has always remained in the possession of Mr. Cabot's descendants, and was engraved for the first time for Hamilton's Works, that were edited by Hon. Henry Cabot Lodge, and published in the Statemen's Series by G. P. Putnam's Sons, in 1885.

In the preface to that admirable edition, Mr. Lodge says:

> The influence of the policy of Washington's administration upon the establishment and development of this great nation of ours cannot be over-estimated. Much of that policy was due to Hamilton alone, and in all parts of it he made himself deeply felt. Hamilton's

greatest work was in creating, forming, and guiding a powerful public opinion in support of a national system, and the sentiment thus brought into being went steadily on, with ever-increasing force, until it prevailed over all its enemies. No statesman in our history has ever swayed so many of the leading men among his contemporaries as Hamilton; and, at the same time, he appealed with his pen to the largest popular audience of any man of his time. He was the first teacher in the school of national politics.

But there is another side to Hamilton's writings which makes them of even wider and more lasting worth than their effect upon the people of the United States. This is their intrinsic merit, as contributions to the philosophy or science of government, as well as to finance and political economy. These were questions much meditated upon at the close of the eighteenth century, and they have engaged the best attention of the civilized world ever since. Hamilton ranks as one of the great thinkers in the days when political economy and the huge mechanism of modern finance came into being. He stands conspicuous in that all-important period, and in that broad field of thought, side by side with such men as Turgot, Pitt, and Adam Smith; and he does not suffer by comparison with these contemporaries, either in force and originality of ideas, or in practical success. He studied Adam Smith, and then wrote the Report on Manufactures, developing the theory as to the protection of nascent industries in its application to the United States, and standing firmly on the doctrine that this was a question which each nation must decide for itself.

MANUFACTURES.

Communicated to the House of Representatives, Dec. 5, 1791.

THE Secretary of the Treasury, in obedience to the order of the House of Representatives, of the 15th day of January, 1790, has applied his attention, at as early a period as his other duties would permit, to the subject of Manufactures, and particularly to the means of promoting such as will tend to render the United States independent on foreign nations for military and other essential supplies; and he thereupon respectfully submits the following report:

The expediency of encouraging manufactures in the United States, which was not long since deemed very questionable, appears at this time to be pretty generally admitted. The embarrassments which have obstructed the progress of our external trade, have led to serious reflections on the necessity of enlarging the sphere of our domestic commerce. The restrictive regulations, which, in foreign markets, abridge the vent of the increasing surplus of our agricultural produce, serve to beget an earnest desire that a more extensive demand for that surplus may be created at home; and the complete success which has rewarded manufacturing enterprise in some valuable branches, conspiring with the promising symptoms which attend some less mature essays in others, justify a hope that the obstacles to the growth of this species of industry are less formidable than they were apprehended to be, and that it is not difficult to find, in its further extension, a full indemnification for any external disadvantages, which are or may be experienced, as well as an accession of resources favorable to national independence and safety.

There still are, nevertheless, respectable patrons of opinions unfriendly to the encouragement of manufactures. The following are, substantially, the arguments by which these opinions are defended:

"In every country (say those who entertain them) agriculture is the most beneficial and productive object of human industry. This position, generally if not universally true, applies with peculiar emphasis to the United States, on account of their immense tracts of fertile territory, uninhabited and unimproved. Nothing can afford so advantageous an employment for capital and labor, as the conversion of this extensive wilderness into cultivated farms. Nothing, equally with this, can contribute to the population, strength, and real riches of the country.

"To endeavor, by the extraordinary patronage of government, to accelerate the growth of manufactures, is, in fact, to endeavor, by force and art, to transfer the natural current of industry from a more to a less beneficial channel. Whatever has such a tendency must necessarily be unwise; indeed it can hardly ever be wise in a government to attempt to give a direction to the industry of its citizens. This, under the quick-sighted guidance of private interest, will, if left to itself, infallibly find its own way to the most profitable employment; and it is by such employment, that the public prosperity will be most effectually promoted. To leave industry to itself, therefore, is, in almost every case, the soundest as well as the simplest policy.

"This policy is not only recommended to the United States by considerations which effect all nations; it is, in a manner, dictated to them by the imperious force of a very peculiar situation. The smallness of their population compared with their territory; the constant allurements to emigration from the settled to the unsettled parts of the country; the facility with which the less independent condition of an artisan can be exchanged for the more independent condition of a farmer, — these and similar causes conspire to produce, and, for a length of time, must continue to occasion, a scarcity of hands for manufacturing occupation, and dearness of labor generally. To these disadvantages for the prosecution of manufactures, a deficiency of pecuniary capital being added, the prospect of a successful competition with the manufactures of Europe, must be regarded as little less than desperate. Extensive manufactures can only be the offspring of a redundant, at least of a full, population. Till the latter shall characterize the situation of this country, 'tis fain to hope for the former.

"If, contrary to the natural course of things, an unseasonable and premature spring can be given to certain fabrics, by heavy duties, prohibitions, bounties, or by other forced expedients, this will only be to sacrifice the interests of the community to those of particular classes. Besides the misdirection of labor, a virtual monopoly will be given to the persons employed on such fabrics; and an enhancement of price, the inevitable consequence of every monopoly, must be defrayed at the expense of the other parts of society. It is far preferable that those persons should be engaged in the cultivation of the earth, and that we should procure in exchange for its productions, the commodities with which foreigners are able to supply us in greater perfection and upon better terms."

This mode of reasoning is founded upon facts and principles which have certainly respectable pretensions. If it had governed the conduct of nations more generally than it has done, there is room to suppose that it might have carried them faster to prosperity and greatness than they have attained by the pursuit of maxims too widely opposite. Most general theories, however, admit of numerous exceptions, and there are few, if any, of the political kind, which do not blend a considerable portion of error with the truths they inculcate.

In order to an accurate judgment how far that which has been just stated ought to be deemed liable to a similar imputation, it is necessary to advert carefully to the considerations which plead in favor of manufactures, and which appear to recommend the special and positive encouragement of them in certain cases and under certain reasonable limitations.

It ought readily to be conceded that the cultivation of the earth, as the primary and most certain source of national supply, as the immediate and chief source of subsistence to man, as the principal source of those materials which constitute the nutriment of other kinds of labor, as including a state most favorable to the freedom and independence of the human mind — one, perhaps, most conducive to the multiplication of the human species, has intrinsically a strong claim to pre-eminence over every other kind of industry.

But that it has a title to anything like an exclusive predilection in any country, ought to be admitted with great caution; that it is even more productive than every other branch of industry, requires more evidence than has yet been given in support of the position. That its real interests, precious and important, as without the help of exaggeration they truly are, will be advanced rather than injured by the due encouragement of manufactures, may, it is believed, be satisfactorily demonstrated. And it is also believed that the expediency of such encouragement, in a general view, may be shown to be recommended by the most cogent and persuasive motives of national policy.

It has been maintained that agriculture is not only the most productive, but the only productive, species of industry. The reality of this suggestion, in other respects, has, however, not been verified by any accurate detail of facts and calculations; and the general arguments which are adduced to prove it are subtle and paradoxical, rather than solid or convincing.

Those which maintain its exclusive productiveness are to this effect:

Labor bestowed upon the cultivation of land produces enough not only to replace all the necessary expenses incurred in the business, and to maintain the persons who are employed in it, but to afford, together with the ordinary profit on the stock or capital of the farmer, a net surplus or rent for the landlord or proprietor of the soil. But the labor of artificers does nothing more than replace the stock which employs them (or which furnishes materials, tools, and wages), and yields the ordinary profit upon that stock. It yields nothing equivalent to the rent of land; neither does it add anything to the total value of the whole annual produce of the land and labor of the country. The additional value given to those parts of the produce of land which are wrought into manufactures, is counterbalanced by the value of those other parts of that produce which are consumed by the manufacturers. It can, therefore, only be by saving or parsimony, not by the positive productiveness of their labor, that the classes of artificers can, in any degree, augment the revenue of the society.

To this it has been answered:

1. "That, inasmuch as it is acknowledged that manufacturing labor reproduces a value equal to that which is expended or consumed in carrying it on, and continues in existence the original stock or capital employed, it ought, on that account alone, to escape being considered as wholly unproductive. That, though it should be admitted, as alleged, that the consumption of the product of the soil, by the classes of artificers or manufacturers, is exactly equal to the value added by their labor to the materials upon which it is exerted, yet it would not thence follow that it added nothing to the revenue of the society, or to the aggregate value of the annual produce of its land and labor. If the consumption, for any given period, amounted to a given sum, and the increased value of the produce manufactured, in the same period,

to a like sum, the total amount of the consumption and production, during that period, would be equal to the two sums, and consequently double the value of the agricultural produce consumed, and though the increment of value produced by the classes of artificers should at no time exceed the value of the produce of the land consumed by them, yet there would be, at every moment, in consequence of their labor, a greater value of goods in the market than would exist independent of it."

2. "That the position, that artificers can augment the revenue of a society only by parsimony, is true in no other sense than in one which is equallly applicable to husbandmen or cultivators. It may be alike affirmed of all these classes, that the fund acquired by their labor and destined for their support is not, in an ordinary way, more than equal to it. And hence it will follow that augmentations of the wealth or capital of the community (except in the instances of some extraordinary dexterity or skill) can only proceed, with respect to any of them, from the savings of the more thrifty and parsimonious."

3. "That the annual produce of the land and labor of a country can only be increased in two ways — by some improvement in the productive powers of the useful labor which actually exists within it, or by some increase in the quantity of such labor. That, with regard to the first, the labor of artificers being capable of greater subdivision and simplicity of operation than that of cultivators, it is susceptible, in a proportionably greater degree, of improvement in its productive powers, whether to be derived from an accession of skill or from the application of ingenious machinery; in which particular, therefore, the labor employed in the culture of land can pretend to no advantage over that engaged in manufactures. That, with regard to an augmentation of the quantity of useful labor, this, excluding adventitious circumstances, must depend essentially upon an increase of capital, which again must depend upon the savings made out of the revenues of those who furnish or manage that which is at any time employed, whether in agriculture or in manufactures, or in any other way."

But while the exclusive productiveness of agricultural labor has been thus denied and refuted, the superiority of its productiveness has been conceded without hesitation. As this concession involves a point of considerable magnitude, in relation to maxims of public administration, the grounds on which it rests are worthy of a distinct and particular examination.

One of the arguments made use of in support of the idea may be pronounced both quaint and superficial. It amounts to this: That, in the productions of the soil, nature co-operates with man; and that the effect of their joint labor must be greater than that of the labor of man alone.

This, however, is far from being a necessary inference. It is very conceivable that the labor of man alone, laid out upon a work requiring great skill and art to bring it to perfection, may be more productive, in value, than the labor of nature and man combined, when directed toward more simple operations and objects; and when it is recollected to what an extent the agency of nature, in the application of the mechanical powers, is made auxiliary to the prosecution of manufactures, the suggestion which has been noticed loses even the appearance of plausibility.

It might also be observed, with a contrary view, that the labor employed in agriculture is, in a great measure, periodical and occasional, depending on seasons, and liable to various and long intermissions, while that occupied in many manufactures is constant and regular, extending through the year, embracing, in some instances, night as well as day. It is also probable that there are, among the cultivators of land, more examples of remissness than among artificers. The farmer, from the peculiar fertility of his land, or some other favorable circumstance, may frequently obtain a livelihood, even with a considerable degree of carelessness in the mode of cultivation; but the artisan can with difficulty effect the same object without exerting himself pretty equally with all those who are engaged in the same pursuit. And if it may likewise be assumed as a fact that manufactures open a wider field to exertions of ingenuity than agriculture, it would not be a strained conjecture that the labor employed in the former, being at once more constant, more uniform and more ingenious than that which is employed in the latter, will be found, at the same time, more productive.

But it is not meant to lay stress on observations of this nature; they ought only to serve as a counterbalance to those of a similar complexion. Circumstances so vague and general, as well as so abstract, can afford little instruction in a matter of this kind.

Another, and that which seems to be the principal argument offered for the superior productiveness of agricultural labor, turns upon the allegation that labor employed upon manufactures yields nothing equivalent to the rent of the land, or to that net surplus, as it is called, which accrues to the proprietor of the soil.

But this distinction, important as it has been deemed, appears, rather verbal than substantial.

It is easily discernable that what, in the first instance, is divided into two parts, under the denominations of the ordinary profit of the stock of the farmer and rent to the landlord, is, in the second instance, united under the general appellation of the ordinary profit on the stock of the undertaker; and that this formal or verbal distribution constitutes the whole difference in the two cases. It seems to have been overlooked that the land is itself a stock or capital, advanced or lent by its owner to the occupier or tenant, and that the rent he receives is only the ordinary profit of a certain stock in land, not managed by the proprietor himself, but by another, to whom he lends or lets it, and who, on his part, advances a second capital, to stock and improve the land, upon which he also receives the usual profit. The rent of the landlord and the profit of the farmer are, therefore, nothing more than the ordinary profits of two capitals belonging to two different persons, and united in the cultivation of a farm; as, in the other case, the surplus which arises upon any manufactory, after replacing the expenses of carrying it on, answers to the ordinary profits of one or more capitals engaged in the prosecution of such manufactory. It is said one or more capitals, because, in fact, the same thing which is contemplated in the case of the farm, sometimes happens in that of a manufactory. There is one who furnishes a part of the capital or lends a part of the money by which it is carried on, and another who carries it on with an addition of his own capital. Out of the surplus which remains after defraying expenses, an interest is paid to the money lender, for the portion of the capital furnished by him, which exactly agrees with the rent paid to the landlord; and the residue of that surplus constitutes the profit of the undertaker or manufacturer, and agrees with what is denominated the ordinary profits on the stock of the farmer. Both together make the ordinary profits of two capitals employed in a manufactory; as, in the other case, the rent of the landlord and the revenue of the farmer compose the ordinary profits of two capitals employed in the cultivation of a farm.

The rent, therefore, accruing to the proprietor of the land, far from being a criterion of exclusive productiveness, as has been argued, is no criterion even of superior productiveness. The question must still be whether the surplus, after defraying expenses, of a given capital, employed in the purchase and improvement of a piece of land, is greater or less than that of a like capital, employed in the prosecution of a manufactory; or whether the whole value produced from a given capital, and a given quantity of labor, employed in one way, be greater or less than the whole value produced from an equal capital and an equal quantity of labor, employed in the other way; or rather, perhaps, whether the business of agriculture or that of manufactures will yield the greater product, according to the compound ratio of the quantity of the capital and the quantity of labor which are employed in the one or in the other.

The solution of either of these questions is not easy; it involves numerous and complicated details, depending on an acurate knowledge of the objects to be compared. It is not known that the comparison has ever yet been made upon sufficient data, properly ascertained and analyzed. To be able to make it, on the present occasion, with satisfactory precision, would demand more previous inquiry and investigation than there has been, hitherto, either leisure or opportunity to accomplish.

Some essays, however, have been made toward acquiring the requisite information, which have rather served to throw doubt upon, than to confirm, the hypothesis under examination. But it ought to be acknowledged that they have been too little diversified, and are too imperfect to authorize a definite conclusion, either way; leading rather to probable conjecture than to certain deduction. They render it probable that there are various branches of manufactures, in which a given capital yields a greater total product, and a considerably greater net product, than an equal capital invested in the purchase and improvement of lands; and that there are also some branches, in which both the gross and the net produce will exceed that of agricultural industry, according to a compound ratio of capital and labor. But it is on this last point that there appears to be the greatest room for doubt. It is far less difficult to infer generally, that the net produce of capital engaged in manufacturing enterprises is greater than that of capital engaged in agriculture.

The foregoing suggestions are not designed to inculcate an opinion that manufacturing industry is more productive than that of agriculture. They are intended rather to show that the reverse of this proposition is not ascertained; that the general arguments which are brought to establish it are not satisfactory; and, consequently, that a supposition of the superior productiveness of tillage ought to be no obstacle to listening to any substantial inducements to the encouragement of manufactures, which may be otherwise perceived to exist, through an apprehension that they may have a tendency to divert labor from a more to a less profitable employment.

It is extremely probable that, on a full and accurate development of the matter, on the ground of fact and calculation, it would be discovered that there is no material difference between the aggregate productiveness of the one and of the other kind of industry; and that the propriety of the encouragements which may, in any case, be proposed to be given to either, ought to be determined upon considerations irrelative to any comparison of that nature.

But, without contending for the superior productiveness of manufacturing industry, it may conduce to a better judgment of the policy which ought to be pursued respecting its encouragement, to contemplate the subject under some additional aspects, tending not only to confirm the idea that this kind of industry has been improperly represented as unproductive in itself, but to evince, in addition, that the establishment and diffusion of manufactures have the effect of rendering the total mass of useful and productive labor, in a community, greater than it would otherwise be. In prosecuting this discussion, it may be necessary briefly to resume and review some of the topics which have been already touched.

To affirm that the labor of the manufacturer is unproductive, because he consumes as much of the produce of land as he adds value to the raw material which he manufactures, is not better founded than it would be to affirm that the labor of the farmer, which furnishes materials to the manufacturer, is unproductive, because he consumes an equal value of manufactured articles. Each furnishes a certain portion of the produce of his labor to the other, and each destroys a corresponding portion of the produce of the labor of the other. In the mean time, the maintenance of two citizens, instead of one, is going on; the State has two members instead of one; and they, together, consume twice the value of what is produced from the land.

If, instead of a farmer and artificer, there were a farmer only, he would be under the necessity of devoting a part of his labor to the fabrication of clothing and other articles, which he would procure of the artificer, in the case of there being such a person; and of course, he would be able to devote less labor to the cultivation of his farm, and would draw from it a proportionately less product. The whole quantity of production, in this state of things, in provisions, raw materials, and manufactures, would certainly not exceed in value the amount of what would be produced in provisions and raw materials only, if there were an artificer as well as a farmer.

Again, if there were both an artificer and a farmer, the latter would be left at liberty to pursue exclusively the cultivation of his farm. A greater quantity of provisions and raw materials would, of course, be produced, equal, at least, as has been already observed, to the whole amount of the provisions, raw materials, and manufactures, which would exist in a contrary supposition. The artificer, at the same time, would be going on in the production of manufactured commodities, to an amount sufficient, not only to repay the farmer, in those commodities, for the provisions and materials which were procured from him, but to furnish the artificer himself with a supply of similar commodities for his own use. Thus, then, there would be two quantities or values in existence, instead of one; and the revenue and consumption would be double, in one case, what it would be in the other.

If, in the place of both of these suppositions, there were supposed to be two farmers and no artificer, each of whom applied a part of his labor to the culture of land and another part to the fabrication of manufactures,—in this case, the portion of the labor of both, bestowed upon land, would produce the same quantity of provisions and raw materials only, as would be produced by the entire sum of the labor of one, applied in the same manner; and the portion of the labor of both, bestowed upon manufactures, would produce the same quantity of manufactures only, as would be produced by the entire sum of the labor of one, applied in the same manner. Hence, the produce of the labor of the two farmers would not be greater than the produce of the labor of the farmer and artificer; and hence it results that the labor of the artificer is as positively productive as that of the farmer, and as positively augments the revenue of the society.

The labor of the artificer replaces to the farmer that portion of his labor with which he provides the materials of exchange with the artificer, and which he would otherwise have been compelled to apply to manufactures; and while the artificer thus enables the farmer to enlarge his stock of agricultural industry, a portion of which he purchases for his own use, he also supplies himself with the manufactured articles of which he stands in need. He does still more. Besides this equivalent, which he gives for the portion of agricultural labor consumed by him, and this supply of manufactured commodities for his own consumption, he furnishes still a surplus, which compensates for the use of the capital advanced, either by himself or some other person, for carrying on the business. This is the ordinary profit of the stock employed in the manufactory, and is, in every sense, as effective an addition to the income of society as the rent of land.

The produce of the labor of the artificer, consequently, may be regarded as composed of three parts; one, by which the provisions for his subsistence and the materials for his work are purchased of the farmer; one, by which he supplies himself with manufactured necessaries; and a third, which constitutes the profit on the stock employed. The two last portions seem to have been overlooked in the system which represents manufacturing industry as barren and unproductive.

In the course of the preceding illustrations, the products of equal quantities of the labor of the farmer and artificer have been treated as if equal to each other. But this is not to be understood as intending to assert any such precise equality. It is merely a manner of expression, adopted for the sake of simplicity and perspicuity. Whether the value of the produce of the labor of the farmer be somewhat more or less than that of the artificer, is not material to the main scope of the argument, which, hitherto, has only aimed at showing that the one, as well as the other, occasions a positive augmentation of the total produce and revenue of the society.

It is now proper to proceed a step further, and to enumerate the principal circumstances from which it may be inferred that manufacturing establishments not only occasion a positive augmentation of the produce and revenue of the society, but that they contribute essentially to rendering them greater than they could possibly be without such establishments. These circumstances are:

1. The division of labor.

2. An extension of the use of machinery.

3. Additional employment to classes of the community not ordinarily engaged in business.

4. The promoting of immigration from foreign countries.

5. The furnishi greater scope for the diversity of talents and d spositions, which discriminate men from each other.

6. The affording a more ample and various field for enterprise.

7. The creating, in some instances, a new, and securing, in all, a more certain and steady demand for the surplus produce of the soil.

Each of these circumstances has a considerable influence upon the total mass of industrious effort in a community; together, they add to it a degree of energy and effect which is not easily conceived. Some comments upon each of them, in the order in which they have been stated, may serve to explain their importance.

1. As to the division of labor.

It has justly been observed that there is scarcely anything of greater moment in the economy of a nation than the proper division of labor. The separation of occupations causes each to be carried to a much greater perfection than it could possibly acquire if they were blended. This arises principally from three circumstances:

1st. The greater skill and dexterity naturally resulting from a constant and undivided application to a single object. It is evident that these properties must increase in proportion to the separation and simplification of objects, and the steadiness of the attention devoted to each; and must be less in proportion to the complication of objects, and the number among which the attention is distracted.

2d. The economy of time, by avoiding the loss of it, incident to a frequent transition from one operation to another of a different nature. This depends on various circumstances; the transition itself, the orderly disposition of the implements, machines, and materials employed in the operation to be relinquished, the preparatory steps to the commencement of a new one, the interruption of the impulse which the mind of a workman acquires from being engaged in a particular operation, the distractions, hesitations, and reluctances which attend the passage from one kind of business to another.

3d. An extension of the use of machinery. A man occupied on a single object will have it more in his power, and will be more naturally led to exert his imagination, in devising methods to facilitate and abridge labor, than if he were perplexed by a variety of independent and dissimilar operations. Besides this, the fabrication of machines, in numerous instances, becoming itself a distinct trade, the artist who follows it has all the advantages which have been enumerated for improvement in his particular art; and, in both ways, the invention and application of machinery are extended.

And from these causes united, the mere separation of the occupation of the cultivator from that of the artificer, has the effect of augmenting the productive powers of labor, and with them, the total mass of the produce or revenue of a country. In this single view of the subject, therefore, the utility of artificers or manufacturers, towards promoting an increase of productive industry, is apparent.

2. *As to an extension of the use of machinery, a point which, though partly anticipated, requires to be placed in one or two additional lights.*

The employment of machinery forms an item of great importance in the general mass of national industry. It is an artificial force brought in aid of the natural force of man; and, to all the purposes of labor, is an increase of hands, an accession of strength, unencumbered too by the expense of maintaining the laborer. May it not, therefore, be fairly inferred that those occupations which give the greatest scope to the use of this auxiliary contribute most to the general stock of industrious effort, and, in consequence, to the general product of industry?

It shall be taken for granted, and the truth of the position referred to observation, that manufacturing pursuits are susceptible, in a greater degree, of the application of machinery, than those of agriculture. If so, all the difference is lost to a community which, instead of manufacturing for itself, procures the fabrics requisite to its supply from other countries. The substitution of foreign for domestic manufactures is a transfer to foreign nations of the advantages accruing from the employment of machinery, in the modes in which it is capable of being employed with most utility and to the greatest extent.

The cotton-mill, invented in England, within the last twenty years, is a signal illustration of the general proposition which has been just advanced. In consequence of it, all the different processes for spinning cotton are performed by means of machines, which are put in motion by water, and attended chiefly by women and children — and by a smaller number of persons, in the whole, than are requisite in the ordinary mode of spinning. And it is an advantage of great moment, that the operations of this mill continue with convenience during the night as well as through the day. The prodigious effect of such a machine is easily conceived. To this invention is to be attributed, essentially, the immense progress which has been so suddenly made in Great Britain in the various fabrics of cotton.

3. As to the additional employment of classes of the community not originally engaged in the particular business.

This is not among the least valuable of the names by which manufacturing institutions contribute to augment the general stock of industry and production. In places where these institutions prevail, besides the persons regularly engaged in them, they afford occasional and extra employment to industrious individuals and families, who are willing to devote the leisure resulting from the intermissions of their ordinary pursuits to collateral labors, as a resource for multiplying their acquisitions or their enjoyments. The husbandman himself experiences a new source of profit and support from the increased industry of his wife and daughters, invited and stimulated by the demands of the neighboring manufactories.

Besides this advantage of occasional employment to classes having different occupations, there is another, of a nature allied to it and of a similar tendency. This is the employment of persons who would otherwise be idle, and in many cases a burthen on the community, either from the bias of temper, habit, infirmity of body, or some other cause, indisposing or disqualifying them for the toils of the country. It is worthy of particular remark that, in general, women and children are rendered more useful, and the latter more early useful, by manufacturing establishments, than they would otherwise be. Of the number of persons employed in the cotton manufactories of Great Britain, it is computed that four-sevenths, nearly, are women and children, of whom the greater proportion are children, and many of them of a tender age.

And thus it appears to be one of the attributes of manufactures, and one of no small consequence, to give occasion to the exertion of a greater quantity of industry, even by the same number of persons, where they happen to prevail, than would exist if there were no such establishments.

4. As to the promoting of immigration from foreign countries.

Men reluctantly quit one course of occupation and livelihood for another, unless invited to it by very apparent and proximate advantages. Many who would go from one country to another, if they had a prospect of continuing with more benefit the callings to which they have been educated, will often not be tempted to change their situation by the hope of doing better in some other way. Manufacturers who, listening to the powerful invitations of a better price for their fabrics or their labor, of greater cheapness of provisions, and raw materials, of an exemption from the chief part of the taxes, burthens and restraints which they endure in the Old World, of greater personal independence and consequence, under the operation of a more equal government, and of what is far more precious than mere religious toleration, a perfect quality of religious privileges, would probably flock from Europe to the United States, to pursue their own trades or professions, if they were once made sensible of the advantages they would enjoy, and were inspired with an assurance of encouragement and employment, will, with difficulty, be induced to transplant themselves, with a view to becoming cultivators of land.

If it be true, then, that it is the interest of the United States to open every possible avenue to emigration from abroad, it affords a weighty argument for the encouragement of manufactures; which, for the reasons just assigned, will have the strongest tendency to multiply the inducements to it.

Here is perceived an important resource, not only for extending the population, and with it the useful and productive labor of the country, but likewise for the prosecution of manufactures, without deducting from the number of hands which might otherwise be drawn to tillage, and even for the indemnification of agriculture for such as might happen to be diverted from it. Many, whom manufacturing views would induce to emigrate, would, afterwards, yield to the temptations which the particular situation of this country holds out to agricultural pursuits. And while agriculture would, in other respects, derive many signal and unmingled advantages from the growth of manufacturers, it is a problem whether it would gain or lose, as to the article of the number of persons employed in carrying it on.

5. *As to the furnishing greater scope for the diversity of talents and dispositions, which discriminate men from each other.*

This is a much more powerful means of augmenting the fund of national industry than may at first sight appear. It is a just observation, that minds of the strongest and most active powers for their proper objects fall below mediocrity, and labor without effect if confined to uncongenial pursuits. And it is thence to be inferred, that the results of human exertion may be immensely increased by diversifying its objects. When all the different kinds of industry obtain in a community, each individual can find his proper element, and can call into activity the whole vigor of his nature. And the community is benefited by the services of its respective members, in the manner in which each can serve it with most effect.

If there be anything in a remark often to be met with, namely, that there is, in the genius of the people of this country, a peculiar aptitude for mechanic improvements, it would operate as a forcible reason for giving opportunities to the exercise of that species of talent, by the propagation of manufactures.

6. *As to the affording a more ample and various field for enterprise.*

This is also of greater consequence in the general scale of national exertion than might, perhaps, on a superficial view, be supposed, and has effects not altogether dissimilar from those of the circumstances last noticed. To cherish and stimulate the activity of the human mind, by multiplying the objects of enterprise, is not among the least considerable of the expedients by which the wealth of a nation may be promoted. Even things in themselves not positively advantageous sometimes become so, by their tendency to provoke exertion. Every new scene which is opened to the busy nature of man to rouse and exert itself, is the addition of a new energy to the general stock of effort.

The spirit of enterprise, useful and prolific as it is, must necessarily be contracted or expanded in proportion to the simplicity or variety of the occupations and productions which are to be found in a society. It must be less in a nation of mere cultivators than in a nation of cultivators and merchants; less in a nation of cultivators and merchants than in a nation of cultivators, artificers, and merchants.

7. *As to the creating, in some instances, a new, and securing, in all, a more certain and steady demand for the surplus produce of the soil.*

This is among the most important of the circumstances which have been indicated. It is a principal means by which the establishment of manufactures contributes to an augmentation of the produce or revenue of a country, and has an immediate and direct relation to the prosperity of agriculture.

It is evident that the exertions of the husbandman will be steady or fluctuating, vigorous or feeble, in proportion to the steadiness or fluctuation, adequateness or inadequateness of the markets on which he must depend for the vent of the surplus which may be produced by his labor; and that such surplus, in the ordinary course of things, will be greater or less in the same proportion.

For the purpose of this vent, a domestic market is greatly to be preferred to a foreign one; because it is, in the nature of things, far more to be relied upon.

It is a primary object of the policy of nations to be able to supply themselves with subsistence from their own soils; and manufacturing nations, as far as circumstances permit, endeavor to procure from the same source the raw materials necessary for their own fabrics. This disposition, urged by the spirit of monopoly, is sometimes even carried to an injudicious extreme. It seems not always to be recollected that nations who have neither mines nor manufactures can only obtain the manufactured articles of which they stand in need by an exchange of the products of their soils; and that if those who can best furnish them with such articles are unwilling to give a due course to this exchange, they must, of necessity, make every possible effort to manufacture for themselves; the effect of which is, that the manufacturing nations abridge the natural advantages of their situation through an unwillingness to permit the agricultural countries to enjoy the advantages of theirs, and sacrifice the interests of a mutually beneficial intercourse to the vain project of selling everything and buying nothing.

But it is also a consequence of the policy which has been noted, that the foreign demand for the products of agricultural countries is, in a great degree, rather casual and occasional than certain or constant. To what extent injurious interruptions of the demand for some of the staple commodities of the United States may have been experienced from that cause, must be referred to the judgment of those who are engaged in carrying on the commerce of the country; but it may be safely affirmed that such interruptions are, at times, very inconveniently felt, and that cases not infrequently occur in which the markets are so confined and restricted as to render the demand very unequal to the supply.

Independently, likewise, of the artificial impediments which are created by the policy in question, there are natural causes tending to render the external demand for the surplus of agricultural nations a precarious reliance. The differences of seasons in the countries which are the consumers make immense differences in the produce of their own soils, in different years, and consequently in the degrees of their necessity for foreign supply. Plentiful harvests with them, especially if similar ones occur at the same time in the countries which are the furnishers, occasion, of course, a glut in the markets of the latter.

Considering how fast and how much the progress of new settlements in the United States must increase the surplus produce of the soil, and weighing seriously the tendency of the system which prevails among most of the commercial nations of Europe, whatever dependence may be placed on the force of natural circumstances to counteract the effects of an artificial policy, there appear strong reasons to regard the foreign demand for that surplus as too uncertain a reliance, and to desire a substitute for it in an extensive domestic market.

To secure such a market there is no other expedient than to promote manufacturing establishments. Manufacturers, who constitute the most numerous class, after the cultivators of land, are for that reason the principal consumers of the surplus of their labor.

This idea of an extensive domestic market for the surplus produce of the soil is of the first consequence. It is, of all things, that which most effectually conduces to a flourishing state of agriculture. If the effect of manufactories should be to detach a portion of the hands which would otherwise be engaged in tillage, it might possibly cause a smaller quantity of lands to be under cultivation; but by their tendency to procure a more certain demand for the surplus produce of the soil, they would, at the same time, cause the lands which were in cultivation to be better improved and more productive. And while, by their influence, the condition of each individual farmer would be meliorated, the total mass of agricultural production would probably be increased. For this must evidently depend as much upon the degree of improvement, if not more, than upon the number of acres under culture.

It merits particular observation that the multiplication of manufactories not only furnishes a market for those articles which have been accustomed to be produced in abundance in a country, but it likewise creates a demand for such as were either unknown or produced in inconsiderable quantities. The bowels as well as the surface of the earth are ransacked for articles which were before neglected. Animals, plants, and minerals acquire a utility and a value which were before unexplored.

The foregoing considerations seem sufficient to establish, as general propositions, that it is the interest of nations to diversify the industrious pursuits of the individuals who compose them; that the establishment of manufactures is calculated not only to increase the general stock of useful and productive labor, but even to improve the state of agriculture in particular,—certainly to advance the interests of those who are engaged in it. There are other views that will be hereafter taken of the subject, which it is conceived will serve to confirm these inferences.

III. Previous to a further discussion of the objections to the encouragement of manufactures, which have been stated, it will be of use to see what can be said, in reference to the particular situation of the United States, against the conclusions appearing to result from what has been already offered.

It may be observed, and the idea is of no inconsiderable weight, that however true it might be that a State, which, possessing large tracts of vacant and fertile territory, was at the same time secluded from foreign commerce, would find its interest and the interest of agriculture in diverting a part of its population from tillage to manufactures, yet it will not follow that the same is true of a State which, having such vacant and fertile territory, has at the same time ample opportunity of procuring from abroad, on good terms, all the fabrics of which it stands in need for the supply of its inhabitants. The power of doing this at least secures the great advantage of a division of labor, leaving the farmer free to pursue, exclusively, the culture of his land, and enabling him to procure with its products the manufactured supplies requisite either to his wants or to his enjoyments. And though it should be true that, in settled countries, the diversification of industry is conducive to an increase in the productive powers of labor, and to an augmentation of revenue and capital, yet it is scarcely conceivable that there can be anything of so solid and permanent advantage to an uncultivated and unpeopled country as to convert its wastes into cultivated and inhabited districts. If the revenue, in the mean time, should be less, the capital, in the event, must be greater.

To these observations the following appears to be a satisfactory answer:

1. If the system of perfect liberty to industry and commerce

were the prevailing system of nations, the arguments which dissuade a country, in the predicament of the United States, from the zealous pursuit of manufactures would doubtless have great force. It will not be affirmed that they might not be permitted, with few exceptions, to serve as a rule of national conduct. In such a state of things, each country would have the full benefit of its peculiar advantages to compensate for its deficiencies or disadvantages. If one nation were in a condition to supply manufactured articles on better terms than another, that other might find an abundant indemnification in a superior capacity to furnish the produce of the soil. And a free exchange, mutually beneficial, of the commodities which each was able to supply on the best terms, might be carried on between them, supporting in full vigor the industry of each. And though the circumstances which have been mentioned, and others which will be unfolded hereafter, render it probable that nations, merely agricultural, would not enjoy the same degree of opulence in proportion to their numbers as those which united manufactures with agriculture, yet the progressive improvement of the lands of the former might in the end atone for an inferior degree of opulence in the meantime; and in a case in which opposite considerations are pretty equally balanced, the option ought, perhaps, always to be in favor of leaving industry to its own direction.

But the system which has been mentioned is far from characterizing the general policy of nations. The prevalent one has been regulated by an opposite spirit. The consequence of it is that the United States are, to a certain extent, in the situation of a country precluded from foreign commerce. They can, indeed, without difficulty, obtain from abroad the manufactured supplies of which they are in want; but they experience numerous and very injurious impediments to the emission and vent of their own commodities. Nor is this the case in reference to a single foreign nation only. The regulations of several countries, with which we have the most extensive intercourse, throw serious obstructions in the way of the principal staples of the United States.

In such a position of things, the United States cannot exchange with Europe on equal terms; and the want of reciprocity would render them the victim of a system which would induce them to confine their views to agriculture and refrain from manufactures. A constant and increasing necessity, on their part, for the commodities of Europe, and only a partial and occasional demand for their own, in return, could not but expose them to a state of impoverishment, compared with the opulence to which their political and natural advantages authorize them to aspire.

Remarks of this kind are not made in the spirit of complaint. It is for the nations, whose regulations are alluded to, to judge for themselves whether by aiming at too much they do not lose more than they gain. It is for the United States to consider by what means they can render themselves least dependent on the combinations, right or wrong, of foreign policy.

It is no small consolation that already the measures which have embarrassed our trade have accelerated internal improvements, which, upon the whole, have bettered our affairs. To diversify and extend these improvements is the surest and safest method of indemnifying ourselves for any inconveniencies which those or similar measures have a tendency to beget. If Europe will not take from us the products of our soil, upon terms consistent with our interest, the natural remedy is to contract, as fast as possible, our wants of her.

2. The conversion of their waste into cultivated lands is certainly a point of great moment in the political calculations of the United States. But the degree in which this may possibly be retarded by the encouragement of manufactories does not appear to countervail the powerful inducements to afford that encouragement.

An observation made in another place is of a nature to have great influence upon this question. If it cannot be denied that the interests, even of agriculture, may be advanced more by having such of the lands of a State as are occupied under good cultivation, than by having a greater quantity occupied under a much inferior cultivation; and if manufactories, for the reasons assigned, must be admitted to have a tendency to promote a more steady and vigorous cultivation of the lands occupied than would happen without them, it will follow that they are capable of indemnifying a country for a diminution of the progress of new settlements, and may serve to increase both the capital value and the income of its lands, even though they should abridge the number of acres under tillage.

But it does by no means follow that the progress of new settlements would be retarded by the extension of manufactures. The desire of being an independent proprietor of land is founded on such strong principles in the human breast, that, where the opportunity of becoming so is as great as it is in the United States, the proportion will be small of those whose situations would otherwise lead to it, who would be diverted from it toward manufactures. And it is highly probable, as already intimated, that the accessions of foreigners, who, originally drawn over by manufacturing views, would afterward abandon them for agricultural, would be more than an equivalent for those of our own citizens who might happen to be detached from them.

The remaining objections to a particular encouragement of manufactures in the United States now require to be examined.

One of these turns on the proposition that industry, if left to itself, will naturally find its way to the most useful and profitable employment. Whence it is inferred that manufactures, without the aid of government, will grow up as soon and as fast as the natural state of things and the interest of the community may require.

Against the solidity of this hypothesis, in the full latitude of the terms, very cogent reasons may be offered. These have relation to the strong influence of habit and the spirit of imitation; the fear of want of success in untried enterprises; the intrinsic difficulties incident to first essays toward a competition with those who have previously attained to perfection in the business to be attempted; the bounties, premiums, and other artificial encouragements with which foreign nations second the exertions of their own citizens in the branches in which they are to be rivalled.

Experience teaches that men are often so much governed by what they are accustomed to see and practise, that the simplest and most obvious improvements, in the most ordinary occupations, are adopted with hesitation, reluctance, and by slow gradations. The spontaneous transition to new pursuits, in a community long habituated to different ones, may be expected to be attended with proportionately greater difficulty.

When former occupations ceased to yield a profit adequate to the subsistence of their followers, or when there was an absolute deficiency of employment in them owing to the superabundance of hands, changes would ensue; but these changes would be likely to be more tardy than might consist with the interest either of individuals or of the society. In many cases they would not happen, while a bare support could be insured by an adherence to ancient courses, though a resort to a more profitable employment might be practicable. To produce the desirable changes as early as may be expedient may therefore require the incitement and patronage of government.

The apprehension of failing in new attempts is, perhaps, a more serious impediment. There are dispositions apt to be attracted by the mere novelty of an undertaking; but these are not always those best calculated to give it success. To this it is of importance that the confidence of cautious, sagacious capitalists, both citizens and foreigners, should be excited. And to inspire this description of persons with confidence, it is essential that they should be made to see in any project which is new — and for that reason alone, if for no other, precarious — the prospect of such a degree of countenance and support from government, as may be capable of overcoming the obstacles inseparable from first experiments.

The superiority antecedently enjoyed by nations who have preoccupied and perfected a branch of industry, constitutes a more formidable obstacle than either of those which have been mentioned, to the introduction of the same branch into a country in which it did not before exist. To maintain, between the recent establishments of one country and the long-matured establishments of another country, a competition upon equal terms, both as to quality and price, is, in most cases, impracticable. The disparity in the one, or in the other, or in both must necessarily be so considerable as to forbid a successful rivalship, without the extraordinary aid and protection of government.

But the greatest obstacle of all to the successful prosecution of a new branch of industry in a country in which it was before unknown consists, as far as the instances apply, in the bounties, premiums, and other aids which are granted, in a variety of cases, by the nations in which the establishments to be imitated are previously introduced. It is well known (and particular examples, in the course of this report, will be cited) that certain nations grant bounties on the exportation of particular commodities, to enable their own workmen to undersell and supplant all competitors in the countries to which those commodities are sent. Hence the undertakers of a new manufacture have to contend, not only with the natural disadvanages of a new undertaking, but with the gratuities and remunerations which other governments bestow. To be enabled to contend with success, it is evident that the interference and aid of their own governments are indispensible.

Combinations by those engaged in a particular branch of business in one country to frustrate the first efforts to introduce it into another, by temporary sacrifices, recompensed, perhaps, by extraordinary indemnifications of the government of such country, are believed to have existed, and are not to be regarded as destitute of probability. The existence or assurance of aid from the government of the country in which the business is to be introduced may be essential to fortify adventurers against the dread of such combinations; to defeat their efforts, if formed; and to prevent their being formed, by demonstrating that they must in the end prove fruitless.

Whatever room there may be for an expectation that the industry of a people, under the direction of private interest, will, upon equal terms, find out the most beneficial employment for itself, there is none for a reliance that it will struggle against the force of unequal terms, or will, of itself, surmount all the advantitious barriers to a successful competition which may have been erected, either by the advantages naturally acquired from practice and previous possession of the ground, or by those which may have sprung from positive regulations and an artificial policy. This general reflection might alone suffice as an answer to the objection under examination, exclusively of the weighty considerations which have been particularly urged.

The objections to the pursuit of manufactures in the United States, which next present themselves to discussion, represent an impracticability of success, arising from three causes: scarcity of hands, dearness of labor, want of capital.

The two first circumstances are, to a certain extent, real; and within due limits, ought to be admitted as obstacles to the success of manufacturing enterprise in the United States. But there are various considerations which lessen their force, and tend to afford an assurance that they are not sufficient to prevent the advantageous prosecution of many very useful and extensive manufactories.

With regard to scarcity of hands, the fact itself must be applied with no small qualification to certain parts of the United States. There are large districts which may be considered as pretty fully peopled, and which, notwithstanding a continual drain for distant settlement, are thickly interspersed with flourishing and increasing towns. If these districts have not already reached the point at which the complaint of scarcity of hands ceases, they are not remote from it, and are approaching fast towards it; and having, perhaps, fewer attractions to agriculture than some other parts of the Union they exhibit a proportionably stronger tendency towards other kinds of industry. In these districts may be discerned no inconsiderable maturity for manufacturing establishments.

But there are circumstances which have been already noticed, with another view, that materially diminish, everywhere, the effect of a scarcity of hands. These circumstances are: The great use which can be made of women and children, on which point a very pregnant and instructive fact has been mentioned — the vast extension given by late improvements to the employment of machines — which, substituting the agency of fire and water, has prodigiously lessened the necessity for manual labor; the employment of persons ordinarily engaged in other occupations during the seasons or hours of leisure, which, besides giving occasion to the exertion of a greater quantity of labor, by the same number of persons, and thereby increasing the general stock of labor, as has been elsewhere remarked, may also be taken into calculation, as a resource for obviating the scarcity of hands; lastly, the attraction of foreign emigrants. Whoever inspects, with a careful eye, the composition of our towns, will be made sensible to what an extent this resource may be relied upon. This exhibits a large proportion of ingenious and valuable workmen, in different arts and trades, who, by expatriating from Europe, have improved their own condition and added to the industry and wealth of the United States. It is a natural inference, from the experience we have already had, that, as soon as the United States shall present the countenance of a serious prosecution of manufacturers, as soon as foreign artists shall be made sensible that the state of things here affords a moral certainty of employment and encouragement, competent numbers of European workmen will transplant themselves, effectually to insure the success of the design. How, indeed, can it otherwise happen, considering the various and powerful inducements which the situation of this country offers — addressing themselves to so many strong passions and feelings, to so many general and particular interests.

It may be affirmed, therefore, in respect to hands for carrying on manufactures, that we shall, in a great measure, trade upon a foreign stock, reserving our own for the cultivation of our lands and the manning of our ships, as far as character and circumstances shall incline. It is not unworthy of remark that the objection to the success of manufacturers, deduced from the scarcity of hands, is alike applicable to trade and navigation, and yet these are perceived to flourish, without any sensible impediment from that cause.

As to the dearness of labor (another of the obstacles alleged), this has relation principally to two circumstances; one, that which has just been discussed, of the scarcity of hands; the other, the greatness of profits.

As far as it is a consequence of a scarcity of hands, it is mitigated by all the considerations which have been adduced as lessening that deficiency. It is certain, too, that the disparity in this respect, between some of the most manufacturing parts of Europe and a large proportion of the United States is not nearly so great as is commonly imagined. It is also much less in regard to artificers and manufacturers than in regard to country laborers; and while a careful comparison shows that there is, in this particular, much exaggeration, it is also evident that the effect of the degree of disparity which does truly exist, is diminished in proportion to the use which can be made of machinery.

To illustrate this last idea, let it be supposed that the difference of price, in two countries, of a given quantity of manual labor requisite to the fabrication of a given article, is as ten, and that some mechanic power is introduced into both countries, which, performing half the necessary labor, leaves only half to be done by hand; it is evident that the difference in the cost of the fabrication of the article in question, in the two countries, as far as it is connected with the price of labor, will be reduced from ten to five, in consequence of the introduction of that power.

This circumstance is worthy the most particular attention. It diminishes immensely one of the objections most strenuously urged against the success of manufactures in the United States.

To procure all such machines as are known in any part of Europe can only require a proper provision and due pains. The knowledge of several of the most important of them is already possessed. The preparation of them here is, in most cases, practicable on nearly equal terms. As far as they depend on water, some superiority of advantages may be claimed, from the uncommon variety and greater cheapness of situations adapted to mill-seats, with which different parts of the United States abound.

So far as the dearness of labor may be a consequence of the

greatness of profits in any branch of business, it is no obstacle to its success. The undertaker can afford to pay the price.

There are grounds to conclude that undertakers of manufactures in this country can, at this time, afford to pay higher wages to the workmen they may employ than are paid to similar workmen in Europe. The prices of foreign fabrics in the market of the United States, which will for a long time regulate the prices of domestic ones, may be considered as compounded of the following ingredients: The first cost of materials, including the taxes, if any, which are paid upon them where they are made; the expense of grounds, buildings, machinery, and tools; the wages of the persons employed in the manufactory; the profits on the capital of stock employed; the commissions of agents to purchase them where they are made; the expense of transportation to the United States, including insurance and other incidental charges; the taxes or duties, if any, and fees of office which are paid on their exportation; the taxes or duties and fees of office which are paid on their importation.

As to the first of these items, the cost of materials, the advantage, upon the whole, is at present on the side of the United States; and the difference in their favor must increase in proportion as a certain and extensive domestic demand shall induce the proprietors of land to devote more of their attention to the production of these materials. It ought not to escape observation, in a comparison on this point, that some of the principal manufacturing countries of Europe are much more dependent on foreign supply for the materials of their manufactures than would be the United States, who are capable of supplying themselves with a greater abundance, as well as a greater variety of the requisite materials.

As to the second item, the expense of grounds, buildings, machinery, and tools, an equality at least may be assumed, since advantages in some particulars will counterbalance temporary disadvantages in others.

As to the third item, or the article of wages, the comparison certainly turns against the United States; though, as before observed, not in so great a degree as commonly supposed.

The fourth item is alike applicable to the foreign and to the domestic manufacture. It is, indeed, more properly a result than a particular to be compared.

But, with respect to all the remaining items, they are alone applicable to the foreign manufacture, and, in the strictest sense, extraordinaries, constituting a sum of extra charge on the foreign fabric which cannot be estimated at less than from fifteen to thirty per cent on the cost of it at the manufactory.

This sum of extra charge may confidently be regarded as more than a counterpoise for the real difference in the price of labor; and is a satisfactory proof that manufactures may prosper in defiance of it in the United States.

To the general allegation, connected with the circumstances of scarcity of hands and dearness of labor, that extensive manufactures can only grow out of a redundant or full population, it will be sufficient to answer generally, that the fact has been otherwise. That the situation alleged to be an essential condition of success, has not been that of several nations, at periods when they had already attained to maturity in a variety of manufactures.

The supposed want of capital for the prosecution of manufactures in the United States is the most indefinite of the objections which are usually opposed to it.

It is very difficult to pronounce anything precise concerning the real extent of the moneyed capital of a country, and still more concerning the proportion which it bears to the objects that invite the employment of capital. It is not less difficult to pronounce how far the effect of any given quantity of money, as capital, or, in other words, as a medium for circulating the industry and property of a nation, may be increased by the very circumstance of the additional motion which is given to it, by new objects of employment. That effect, like the momentum of descending bodies, may not improperly be represented as in a compound ratio to mass and velocity. It seems pretty certain, that a given sum of money, in a situation in which the quick impulses of commercial activity were little felt, would appear inadequate to the circulation of as great a quantity of industry and property, as in one in which their full influence was experienced.

It is not obvious why the same objection might not as well be made to external commerce as to manufactures, since it is manifest that our immense tracts of land, occupied and unoccupied, are capable of giving employment to more capital than is actually bestowed upon them. It is certain that the United States offer a vast field for the advantageous employment of capital; but it does not follow that there will not be found, in one way or another, a sufficient fund for the successful prosecution of any species of industry which is likely to prove truly beneficial.

The following considerations are of a nature to remove all inquietude on the score of want of capital:

The introduction of banks, as has been shown on another occasion, has a powerful tendency to extend the active capital of a country. Experience of the utility of these institutions is multiplying them in the United States. It is probable that they will be established wherever they can exist with advantage; and wherever they can be supported, if administered with prudence; they will add new energies to all pecuniary operations.

The aid of foreign capital may safely, and with considerable latitude, be taken into calculation. Its instrumentality has been long experienced in our external commerce; and it has begun to be felt in various other modes. Not only our funds, but our agriculture, and other internal improvements, have been animated by it. It has already, in a few instances, extended even to our manufactures.

It is a well-known fact that there are parts of Europe which have more capital than profitable domestic objects of employment. Hence, among other proofs, the large loans continually furnished to foreign states. And it is equally certain, that the capital of other parts may find more profitable employment in the United States than at home. And, notwithstanding there are weighty inducements to prefer the employment of capital at home, even at less profit, to an investment of it abroad, though with greater gain, yet these inducements are overruled, either by a deficiency of employment, or by a very material difference in profit. Both these causes operate to produce a transfer of foreign capital to the United States. It is certain, that various objects in this country hold out advantages, which are with difficulty to be equalled elsewhere; and under the increasingly favorable impressions which are entertained of our government, the attractions will become more and more strong. These impressions will prove a rich mine of prosperity to the country if they are confirmed and strengthened by the progress of our affairs. And, to secure this advantage, little more is now necessary than to foster industry, and cultivate order and tranquillity at home and abroad.

It is not impossible, that there may be persons disposed to look, with a jealous eye, on the introduction of foreign capital, as if it were an instrument to deprive our own citizens of the profits of our own industry; but, perhaps, there never could be a more unreasonable jealousy. Instead of being viewed as a rival, it ought to be considered as a most valuable auxiliary, conducing to put in motion a greater quantity of productive labor, and a greater portion of useful enterprise than could exist without it. It is at least evident, that, in a country situated like the United States, with an infinite fund of resources yet to be unfolded, every farthing of foreign capital which is laid out in internal meliorations, and in industrial establishments of a permanent nature, is a precious acquisition.

And, whatever be the objects which originally attract foreign capital, when once introduced, it may be directed towards any purpose of beneficial exertion which is desired. And to detain it among us, there can be no expedient so effectual, as to enlarge the sphere within which it may be usefully employed; though introduced merely with views to speculations in the funds, it may afterwards be rendered subservient to the interests of agriculture, commerce, and manufactures.

But the attraction of foreign capital for the direct purpose of manufactures, ought not to be deemed a chimerical expectation. There are already examples of it, as remarked in another place. And the examples, if the disposition be cultivated, can hardly fail to multiply. There are also instances of another kind, which serve to strengthen the expectation. Enterprises for improving the public communications, by cutting canals, opening the obstructions in rivers, and erecting bridges, have received very material aid from the same source.

When the manufacturing capitalist of Europe shall advert to the many important advantages which have been intimated in the course of this report, he cannot but perceive very powerful inducements to a transfer of himself and his capital to the United States. Among the reflections which a most interesting peculiarity of situation is calculated to suggest, it cannot escape his observation, as a circumstance of moment in the calculation, that the progressive population and improvement of the United States insure a continually increasing domestic demand for the fabrics which he shall produce, not to be effected by any external casualties or vicissitudes.

But, while there are circumstances sufficiently strong to authorize a considerable degree of reliance on the aid of foreign capital, towards the attainment of the object in view, it is satisfactory to have good grounds of assurance, that there are domestic resources of themselves adequate to it. It happens that there is a species of capital, actually existing in the United States, which relieves from all inquietude on the score of want of capital. This is the funded debt. The effect of a funded debt, as a species of capital, has been noticed upon a former occasion; but a more particular elucidation of the point seems to be required by the stress which is here laid upon it. This shall, accordingly, be attempted.

Public funds answer the purpose of capital, from the estimation in which they are usually held by moneyed men; and, consequently, from the ease and despatch with which they can be turned into money. This capacity of prompt convertibility into money causes a transfer of stock to be, in a great number of cases, equivalent to a payment in coin. And where it does not happen to suit the party who is to receive to accept a transfer of stock, the party who is to pay is never at a loss to find, elsewhere, a purchaser of his stock, who will furnish him, in lieu of it, with the coin of which he stands in need.

Hence, in a sound and settled state of the public funds, a man possessed of a sum in them can embrace any scheme of business which offers, with as much confidence as if he were possessed of an equal sum in coin.

This operation of public funds as capital is too obvious to be denied; but it is objected to the idea of their operating as an augmentation of the capital of the community, that they serve to occasion the destruction of some other capital to an equal amount. The capital, which alone they can be supposed to destroy, must consist of:

The annual revenue, which is applied to the payment of interest on the debt, and to the gradual redemption of the principal; the amount of the coin which is employed in circulating the funds, or, in other words, in effecting the different alienations which they undergo.

But the following appears to be the true and accurate view of this matter:

1st. As to the point of the annual revenue requisite for payment of interest and redemption of principal.

As a determinate proportion will tend to perspicuity in the reasoning, let it be supposed, that the annual revenue to be applied, corresponding with the modification of the six per cent stock of the United States, is in the ratio of eight upon the hundred; that is, in the first instance, six on account of interest, and two on account of principal.

Thus far, it is evident that the capital destroyed, to the capital created, would bear no greater proportion than eight to one hundred. There would be withdrawn, from the total mass of other capitals, a sum of eight dollars to be paid to the public creditor; while he would be possessed of a sum of one hundred dollars, ready to be applied to any purpose, to be embarked in any enterprise which might appear to him eligible. Here, then, the augmentation of capital, or the excess of that which is produced beyond that which is destroyed, is equal to ninety-two dollars.

To this conclusion it may be objected, that the sum of eight dollars is to be withdrawn annually, until the whole hundred is extinguished; and it may be inferred, that, in process of time, a capital will be destroyed equal to that which is at first created.

But it is nevertheless true, that, during the whole of the interval between the creation of the capital of one hundred dollars, and its reduction to a sum not greater than that of the annual revenue appropriated to its redemption, there will be a greater active capital in existence than if no debt had been contracted. The sum drawn from other capitals in any one year will not exceed eight dollars; but there will be, at every instant of time during the whole period in question, a sum corresponding with so much of the principal as remains unredeemed, in the hands of some person or other, employed, or ready to be employed, in some profitable undertaking. There will, therefore, constantly be more capital in capacity to be employed, than capital taken from employment. The excess, for the first year, has been stated to be ninety-two dollars; it will diminish yearly; but there will always be an excess, until the principal of the debt is brought to a level with the redeeming annuity; that is, in the case which has been assumed, by way of example, to eight dollars. The reality of this excess becomes palpable, if it be supposed, as often happens, that the citizen of a foreign country imports into the United States one hundred dollars for the purchase of an equal sum of public debt,—here is an absolute augmentation of the mass of circulating coin to the extent of one hundred dollars. At the end of the year the foreigner is presumed to draw back eight dollars, on account of his principal and interest, but he still leaves ninety-two of his original deposit in circulation, as he, in like manner, leaves eighty-four at the end of the second year, drawing back, then, also, the annuity of eight dollars. And thus the matter proceeds, the capital left in circulation diminishing each year, and coming nearer to the level of the annuity drawn back. There are, however, some differences in the ultimate operation of the part of the debt which is purchased by foreigners, and that which remains in the hands of citizens. But the general effect in each case, though in different degrees, is to add to the active capital of the country.

Hitherto, the reasoning has proceeded on a concession of the position, that there is a destruction of some other capital, to the extent of the annuity appropriated to the payment of the interest and the redemption of the principal of the debt; but in this too much has been conceded. There is, at most, a temporary transfer of some other capital, to the amount of the annuity, from those who pay, to the creditor who receives; which he again restores to the circulation, to resume the offices of a capital. This he does either immediately, by employing the money in some branch of industry, or mediately, by lending it to some other person, who does so employ it, or by spending it on his own maintenance. In either supposition, there is no destruction of capital; there is nothing more than a suspension of its motion for a time—that is, while it is passing from the hands of those who pay into the public coffers, and thence, through the public creditor, into some other channel of circulation. When the payments of interest are periodical and quick, and made by the instrumentality of banks, the diversion or suspension of capital may almost be denominated momentary. Hence the deduction, on this account, is far less than it at first sight appears to be.

There is, evidently, as far as regards the annuity, no destruction or transfer of any other capital than that portion of the income of each individual which goes to make up the annuity. The land which furnishes the farmer with the sum which he is to contribute, remains the same; and the like may be observed of other capitals. Indeed, as far as the tax, which is the object of contribution (as frequently happens, when it does not oppress by its weight), may have been a motive to greater exertion in any occupation; it may even serve to increase the contributory capital. This idea is not without importance in the general view of the subject.

It remains to see what further deduction ought to be made from the capital which is created, by the existence of the debt, on account of the coin which is employed in its circulation. This is susceptible of much less precise calculation than the article which has been just discussed. It is impossible to say what proportion of coin is necessary to carry on the alienations which any species of property usually undergoes. The quantity, indeed, varies according to circumstances. But it may still, without hesitation, be pronounced, from the quickness of the rotation, or rather, of the transitions, that the medium of circulation always bears but a small proportion to the amount of the property circulated. And it is thence satisfactorily deducible, that the coin employed in the negotiations of the funds, and which serves to give them activity, as capital, is incomparably less than the sum of the debt negotiated for the purpose of business.

It ought not, however, to be omitted, that the negotiation of the funds becomes itself a distinct business, which employs, and, by employing, diverts, a portion of the circulating coin from other pursuits. But making due allowance for this circumstance, there is no reason to conclude that the effect of the diversion of coin, in the whole operation, bears any considerable proportion to the amount of the capital to which it gives activity. The sum of the debt in circulation is continually at the command of any useful enterprise; the coin itself, which circulates it, is never more than momentarily suspended from its ordinary functions. It experiences an incessant and rapid flux and reflux, to and from the channels of industry, to those of speculations in the funds.

There are strong circumstances in confirmation of this theory. The force of moneyed capital which has been displayed in Great Britain, and the height to which every species of industry has grown up under it, defy a solution, from the quantity of coin which that kingdom has ever possessed. Accordingly, it has been coeval with its funding system, the prevailing opinion of the men of business, and of the generality of the most sagacious theorists of that country, that the operation of the public funds, as capital, has contributed to the effect in question. Among ourselves, appearances, thus far, favor the same conclusion. Industry, in general, seems to have been re-animated. There are symptoms indicating an extension of our commerce. Our navigation has certainly, of late, had a considerable spring; and there appears to be, in many parts of the Union, a command of capital which till lately, since the Revolution, at least, was unknown. But it is, at the same time, to be acknowledged that other circumstances have concurred (and in a great degree) in producing the present state of things, and that the appearances are not yet sufficiently decisive to be entirely relied upon.

In the question under discussion, it is important to distinguish between an absolute increase of capital, or an accession of real wealth and an artificial increase of capital, as an engine of business, or as an instrument of industry and commerce. In the first sense, a funded debt has no pretensions to being deemed an increase of capital; in the last, it has pretensions which are not easy to be controverted. Of a similar nature is bank credit; and, in an inferior degree, every species of private credit.

But though a funded debt is not, in the first instance, an absolute increase of capital, or an augmentation of real wealth, yet, by serving as a new power in the operations of industry, it has, within certain bounds, a tendency to increase the real wealth of a community, in like manner as money, borrowed by a thrifty farmer to be laid out in the improvement of his farm, may, in the end, add to his stock of real riches.

There are respectable individuals who, from a just aversion to an accumulation of public debt, are unwilling to concede to it any kind of utility; who can discern no good to alleviate the ill with which they suppose it pregnant; who cannot be persuaded that it ought, in any sense, to be viewed as an increase of capital, lest it should be inferred that the more the debt the more the capital, the greater the burthens the greater the blessings of the community.

But it interests the public councils to estimate every object as it truly is; to appreciate how far the good in any measure is compensated by the ill, or the ill by the good; either of them is seldom unmixed.

Neither will it follow that an accumulation of debt is desirable, because a certain degree of it operates as capital. There may be a plethora in the political as in the natural body; there may be a state of things in which any such artificial capital is unnecessary. The debt, too, may be swelled to such a size as that the greatest part of it may cease to be useful as a capital, serving only to pamper the dissipation of idle and dissolute individuals; as that the sums required to pay the interest upon it may become oppressive, and beyond the means which a government can employ, consistently with its tranquillity, to raise them; as that the resources of taxation to face the debt may have been strained too far to admit of extensions adequate to exigencies which regard the public safety.

Where this critical point is, cannot be pronounced; but it is impossible to believe that there is not such a point.

And as the vicissitudes of nations beget a perpetual tendency to the accumulation of debt, there ought to be, in every government, a perpetual, anxious, and unceasing effort to reduce that which at any time exists, as fast as shall be practicable, consistently with integrity and good faith.

Reasonings on a subject comprehending ideas so abstract and complex, so little reducible to a precise calculation, as those which enter into the question just discussed, are always attended with a danger of running into fallacies. Due allowance ought, therefore, to be made for this possibility. But, as far as the nature of the subject admits of it, there appears to be satisfactory ground for a belief that the public funds operate as a resource of capital to the citizens of the United States; and, if they are a resource at all, it is an extensive one.

To all the arguments which are brought to evince the impracticability of success in manufacturing establishments in the United States, it might have been a sufficient answer to have referred to the experience of what has been already done. It is certain that several important branches have grown up and flourished, with a rapidity which surprises, affording an encouraging assurance of success in future attempts. Of these it may not be improper to enumerate the most considerable.

1. *Of Skins.* Tanned and tawed leather, dressed skins, shoes, boots, and slippers, harness and saddlery of all kinds, portmanteaus and trunks, leather breeches, gloves, muffs and tippets, parchment and glue.

2. *Of Iron.* Bar and sheet iron, steel, nail rods and nails, implements of husbandry, stoves, pots and other household utensils, the steel and iron work of carriages, and for ship-building, anchors, scale beams and weights, and various tools of artificers, arms of different kinds; though the manufacture of these last has diminished for want of a demand.

3. *Of Wood.* Ships, cabinet wares, and turnery, wool and cotton cards, and other machinery for manufactures and husbandry, mathematical instruments, coopers' wares of every kind.

4. *Of Flax and Hemp.* Cables, sail cloth, cordage, twine and pack thread.

5. Bricks and coarse tiles, and potters' wares.

6. Ardent spirits and malt liquors.

7. Writing and printing paper, sheathing and wrapping paper, pasteboard, fullers' or press papers, paperhangings.

8. Hats of fur and wool, and mixtures of both, women's stuff and silk shoes.

9. Refined sugars.

10. Oils of animals and seeds, soap, spermaceti and tallow candles.

11. Copper and brass wires, particularly utensils for distillers, sugar refiners, and brewers; andirons and other articles for household use, philosophical apparatus.

12. Tin wares for most purposes of ordinary use.

13. Carriages of all kinds.

14. Snuff, chewing and smoking tobacco.

15. Starch and hair powder.

16. Lampblack and other painters' colors.

17. Gunpowder.

Besides manufactories of these articles, which are carried on as regular trades, and have attained to a considerable degree of maturity, there is a vast scene of household manufacturing, which contributes more largely to the supply of the community than could be imagined without having made it an object of particular inquiry. This observation is the pleasing result of the investigation to which the subject of this report has led, and is applicable as well to the Southern as to the Middle and Northern States. Great quantities of coarse cloths, coatings, serges and flannels, linsey woolseys, hosiery of wool, cotton and thread, coarse fustians, jeans and muslins, checked and striped cotton and linen goods, bed-ticks, coverlets and counterpanes, tow linens, coarse shirtings sheetings, towelling, and table linen, and various mixtures of wool and cotton, and of cotton and flax, are made in the household way, and, in many instances, to an extent not only sufficient for the supply of the families in which they are made, but for sale, and even, in some cases, for exportation. It is computed in a number of districts that two-thirds, three-fourths, and even four-fifths of all the clothing of the inhabitants are made by themselves. The importance of so great a progress as appears to have been made in family manufactures, within a few years, both in a moral and political view, renders the fact highly interesting.

Neither does the above enumeration comprehend all the articles that are manufactured, as regular trades. Many others occur, which are equally well established, but which, not being of equal importance, have been omitted. And there are many attempts, still in their infancy, which, though attended with very favorable appearances, could not have been properly comprised in an enumeration of manufactories already established. There are other articles, also, of great importance, which, though strictly speaking, manufactures, are omitted, as being immediately connected with husbandry; such are flour, pot- and pearl-ashes, pitch, tar, turpentine, and the like.

There remains to be noticed an objection to the encouragement of manufactures, of a nature different from those which question the probability of success. This is derived from its supposed tendency to give a monopoly of advantages to particular classes, at the expense of the rest of the community, who, it is affirmed, would be able to procure the requisite supplies of manufactured articles on better terms from foreigners than from our own citizens, and who, it is alleged, are reduced to the necessity of paying an enhanced price for whatever they want, by every measure which obstructs the free competition of foreign commodities.

It is not an unreasonable supposition, that measures which serve to abridge the free competition of foreign articles have a tendency to occasion an enhancement of prices; and it is not to be denied that such is the effect in a number of cases; but the fact does not uniformly correspond with the theory. A reduction of prices has, in several instances, immediately succeeded the establishment of a domestic manufacture. Whether it be that foreign manufacturers endeavor to supplant, by underselling our own, or whatever else be the cause, the effect has been such as is stated, and the reverse of what might have been expected.

But, though it were true that the immediate and certain effect of regulations controlling the competition of foreign with domestic fabrics was an increase of price, it is universally true that the contrary is the ultimate effect with every successful manufacture. When a domestic manufacture has attained to perfection, and has engaged in the prosecution of it a competent number of persons, it invariably becomes cheaper. Being free from the heavy charges which attend the importation of foreign commodities, it can be afforded, and accordingly seldom never fails to be sold cheaper, in process of time, than was the foreign article for which it was a substitute. The internal competition which takes place soon does away with everything like monoply, and by degrees reduces the price of the article to the minimum of a reasonable profit on the capital employed. This accords with the reason of the thing and with experience.

Whence it follows, that it is the interest of a community, with a view to eventual and permanent economy, to encourage the growth of manufactures. In a national view, a temporary enhancement of price must always be well compensated by a permanent reduction of it.

It is a reflection which may with propriety be indulged here, that this eventual diminution of the prices of manufactured articles, which is the result of internal manufacturing establishments, has a direct and very important tendency to benefit agriculture. It enables the farmer to procure, with a smaller quantity of his labor, the manufactured produce of which he stands in need, and consequently increases the value of his income and property.

The objections which are commonly made to the expediency of encouraging and to the probability of succeeding in manufacturing pursuits, in the United States, having now been discussed, the considerations which have appeared in the course of the discussion, recommending that species of industry to the patronage of the government, will be materially strengthened by a few general and some particular topics, which have been naturally reserved for subsequent notice.

1. There seems to be a moral certainty that the trade of a country, which is both manufacturing and agricultural, will be more lucrative and prosperous than that of a country which is merely agricultural.

One reason for this is found in that general effort of nations (which has been already mentioned) to procure from their own soils the articles of prime necessity requisite to their own consumption and use, and which serves to render their demand for a foreign supply of such articles, in a great degree, occasional and contingent. Hence, while the necessities of nations exclusively devoted to agriculture, for the fabrics of manufacturing States, are constant and regular, the wants of the latter for the products of the former are liable to very considerable fluctuations and interruptions. The great inequalities resulting from difference of seasons have been, elsewhere, remarked. This uniformity of demand on one side, and unsteadiness of it on the other, must necessarily have a tendency to cause the general course of the exchange of commodities between the parties to turn to the disadvantage of the merely agricultural States. Peculiarity of situation, a climate and soil adapted to the production of peculiar commodities, may, sometimes, contradict the rule, but there is every reason to believe that it will be found, in the main, a just one.

Another circumstance, which gives a superiority of commercial advantages to States that manufacture as well as cultivate, consists in the more numerous attractions which a more diversified market offers to foreign customers, and in the greater scope which it affords to mercantile enterprise. It is a position of indisputable truth, in commerce, depending too on very obvious reasons, that the greatest resort will ever be to those marts where commodities, while equally abundant, are most various. Each difference of kind holds out an additional inducement; and it is a position not less clear, that the field of enterprise must be enlarged to the merchants of a country, in proportion to the variety as well as the abundance of commodities which they find at home for exportation to foreign markets.

A third circumstance, perhaps not inferior to either of the other two, conferring the superiority which has been stated, has relation to the stagnations of demand for certain commodities, which, at some time or other, interfere more or less with the sale of all. The nation which can bring to the market but few articles is likely to be more quickly and sensibly affected by such stagnations, than one which is always possessed of a great variety of commodities; the former frequently finds too great a proportion of its stock of materials for sale or exchange lying on hand, or is obliged to make injurious sacrifices to supply its wants of foreign articles, which are numerous and urgent in proportion to the smallness of the number of its own. The latter commonly finds itself indemnified by the high prices of some articles, for the low prices of others; and the prompt and advantageous sale of those articles which are in demand enables its merchants the better to wait for a more favorable change in respect to those which are not. There is ground to believe that a difference of situation, in this particular, has immensely different effects upon the wealth and prosperity of nations.

From these circumstances, collectively, two important inferences are to be drawn; one, that there is always a higher probability of a favorable balance of trade, in regard to countries in which manufactures, founded on the basis of a thriving agriculture, flourish, than in regard to those which are confined wholly, or almost wholly, to agriculture; the other (which is also a consequence of the first), that countries of the former description are likely to possess more pecuniary wealth, or money, than those of the latter.

Facts appear to correspond with this conclusion. The importations of manufactured supplies seem invariably to drain the merely agricultural people of their wealth. Let the situation of the manufacturing countries of Europe be compared, in this particular, with that of countries which only cultivate, and the disparity will be striking. Other causes, it is true, help to account for this disparity between some of them; and among these causes, the relative state of agriculture; but between others of them, the most prominent circumstance of dissimilitude arises from the comparative state of manufactures. In corroboration of the same idea, it ought not to escape remark, that the West India Islands, the soils of which are the most fertile, and the nation which, in the greatest degree, supplies the rest of the world with the precious metals, exchange to a loss with almost every other country.

As far as experience at home may guide, it will lead to the same conclusion. Previous to the Revolution, the quantity of coin possessed by the colonies which now compose the United States, appeared to be inadequate to their circulation, and their debt to Great Britain was progressive. Since the Revolution, the States in which manufactures have most increased have recovered fastest from the injuries of the late war, and abound most in pecuniary resources.

It ought to be admitted, however, in this, as in the preceding case, that causes irrelative to the state of manufactures account, in a degree, for the phenomena remarked. The continual progress of new settlements has a natural tendency to occasion an unfavorable balance of trade, though it indemnifies for the inconvenience, by that increase of the national capital which flows from the conversion of waste into improved lands, and the different degrees of external commerce which are carried on by the different States may make material differences in the comparative state of their wealth. The first circumstance has reference to the deficiency of coin and the increase of debt previous to the Revolution; the last to the advantages which the most manufacturing States appear to have enjoyed over the others since the termination of the late war.

But the uniform appearance of an abundance of specie, as the concomitant of a flourishing state of manufactures, and of the reverse, where they do not prevail, afford a strong presumption of their favorable operation upon the wealth of a country.

Not only the wealth, but the independence and security of a

country, appear to be materially connected with the prosperity of manufactures. Every nation, with a view to these great objects, ought to endeavor to possess within itself all the essentials of national supply. These comprise the means of subsistence, habitation, clothing and defence.

The possession of these is necessary to the perfection of the body politic; to the safety as well as to the welfare of the society. The want of either is the want of an important organ of political life and motion; and in the various crises which await a State, it must severely feel the effect of any such deficiency. The extreme embarrassments of the United States during the late war, from an incapacity of supplying themselves, are still matter of keen recollection; a future war might be expected again to exemplify the mischiefs and dangers of a situation to which that incapacity is still, in too great a degree, applicable, unless changed by timely and vigorous exertion. To effect this change, as fast as shall be prudent, merits all the attention and all the zeal of our public councils; 'tis the next great work to be accomplished.

The want of a navy, to protect our external commerce, as long as it shall continue, must render it a peculiarly precarious reliance for the supply of essential articles, and must serve to strengthen prodigiously the arguments in favor of manufactures.

To these general considerations are added some of a more particular nature.

Our distance from Europe, the great fountain of manufactured supply, subjects us, in the existing state of things, to inconvenience and loss, in two ways.

The bulkiness of those commodities, which are the chief productions of the soil, necessarily imposes very heavy charges on their transportation to distant markets. These charges in the cases in which the nations to whom our products are sent maintain a competition in the supply of their own markets, principally fall upon us, and form material deductions from the primitive value of the articles furnished. The charges on manufactured supplies, brought from Europe, are greatly enhanced by the same circumstances of distance. These charges, again, in the cases in which our own industry maintains no competition in our own markets, also principally fall upon us, and are an additional cause of extraordinary deduction from the primitive value of our own products; these being the materials of exchange for the foreign fabrics which we consume.

The equality and moderation of individual property, and the growing settlements of new districts, occasion in this country an unusual demand for coarse manufactures; the charges of which being greater in proportion to their greater bulk augment the disadvantage which has been just described.

As in most countries, domestic supplies maintain a very considerable competition with such foreign productions of the soil as are imported for sale, if the extensive establishment of manufactories in the United States does not create a similar competition in respect to manufactured articles, it appears to be clearly deducible from the considerations which have been mentioned, that they must sustain a double loss in their exchanges with foreign nations, strongly conducive to an unfavorable balance of trade, and very prejudicial to their interests.

These disadvantages press, with no small weight, on the landed interest of the country. In seasons of peace, they cause a serious deduction from the intrinsic value of the products of the soil. In the time of a war, which should either involve ourselves, or another nation possessing a considerable share of our carrying trade, the charges on the transportation of our commodities, bulky as most of them are, could hardly fail to prove a grievous burthen to the farmer, while obliged to depend, in so great a degree as he now does, upon foreign markets for the vent of the surplus of his labor.

As far as the prosperity of the fisheries of the United States is impeded by the want of an adequate market, there arises another special reason for desiring the extension of mnnufactures. Besides the fish, which, in many places, would be likely to make a part of the subsistence of the persons employed, it is known that the oils, bones and skins of marine animals are of extensive use in various manufactures. Hence, the prospect of an additional demand for the produce of the fisheries.

One more point of view only remains, in which to consider the expediency of encouraging manufactures in the United States.

It is not uncommon to meet with an opinion, that though the promoting of manufactures may be the interest of a part of the Union, it is contrary to that of another part. The Northern and Southern regions are sometimes represented as having adverse interests in this respect. Those are called manufacturing, these agricultural States; and a species of opposition is imagined to subsist between the manufacturing and agricultural interests.

This idea of an opposition between those two interests is the common error of the early periods of every country; but experience gradually dissipates it. Indeed they are perceived so often to succor and befriend each other, that they come at length to be considered as one — a supposition which has been frequently abused, and is not universally true. Particular encouragements of particular manufactures may be of a nature to sacrifice the interests of landholders to those of manufacturers; but it is nevertheless a maxim, well established by experience, and generally acknowledged, where there has been sufficient experience, that the aggregate prosperity of manufactures and the aggregate prosperity of agriculture are intimately connected. In the course of the discussion which has had place, various weighty considerations have been adduced, operating in support of that maxim. Perhaps the superior steadiness of the demand of a domestic market, for the surplus of produce of the soil, is, alone, a convincing argument of its truth.

Ideas of a contrariety of interests between the Northern and Southern regions of the Union are, in the main, as unfounded as they are mischievous. The diversity of circumstances, on which such contrariety is usually predicated, authorizes a directly contrary conclusion. Mutual wants constitute one of the strongest links of political connection, and the extent of these bears a natural proportion to the diversity in the means of mutual supply.

Suggestions of an opposite complexion are ever to be deplored, as unfriendly to the steady pursuit of one great common cause, and to the perfect harmony of all the parts.

In proportion as the mind is accustomed to trace the intimate connection of interest which subsists between all the parts of a society united under the same government, the infinite variety of channels will serve to circulate the prosperity of each, to and through the rest, — in that proportion will it be as little apt to be disturbed by solicitudes and apprehensions which originate in local discriminations.

It is a truth, as important as it is agreeable, and one to which it is not easy to imagine exceptions, that everything tending to establish substantial and permanent order in the affairs of a country, to increase the total mass of industry and opulence, is ultimately beneficial to every part of it. On the credit of this great truth, an acquiescence may safely be accorded, from every quarter, to all institutions and arrangements which promise a confirmation of public order and an augmentation of national resource.

But there are more particular considerations which serve to fortify the idea that the encouragement of manufactures is the interest of all parts of the Union. If the Northern and Middle States should be the principal scenes of such establishments, they would immediately benefit the more Southern, by creating a demand for productions, some of which they have in common with the other States, and others, which are either peculiar to them, or more abundant, or of better quality, than elsewhere. These productions, principally, are timber, flax, hemp, cotton, wool, raw silk, indigo, iron, lead, furs, hides, skins, and coal; of these articles, cotton and indigo are peculiar to the Southern States, as are, hitherto, lead and coal; flax and hemp are, or may be, raised in greater abundance there than in the more Northern States; and the wool of Virginia is said to be of better quality than that of any other state — a circumstance rendered the more probable by the reflection, that Virginia embraces the same latitudes with the finest wool countries of Europe. The climate of the South is also better adapted to the production of silk.

The extensive cultivation of cotton can, perhaps, hardly be expected but from the previous establishment of domestic manufactories of the article; and the surest encouragement and vent for the others would result from similar establishments in respect to them.

If, then, it satisfactorily appears, that it is the interest of the United States, generally, to encourage manufactures, it merits particular attention, that there are circumstances which render the present a critical moment for entering with zeal upon the important business. The effort cannot fail to be materially seconded by a considerable and increasing influx of money, in consequence of foreign speculations in the funds, and by the disorders which exist in different parts of Europe.

The first circumstance not only facilitates the execution of manufacturing enterprises, but it indicates them as a necessary means to turn the thing itself to advantage, and to prevent its being eventually an evil. If useful employment be not found for the money of foreigners brought to the country to be invested in purchases of the public debt, it will quickly be re-exported, to defray the expense of an extraordinary consumption of foreign luxuries; and distressing drains of our specie may, hereafter, be experienced, to pay the interest and redeem the principal of the purchased debt.

This useful employment, too, ought to be of a nature to produce solid and permanent improvements. If the money merely serves to give a temporary spring to foreign commerce, as it cannot procure new and lasting outlets for the products of the country, there will be no real or durable advantage gained. As far as it shall find its way in agricultural meliorations, in opening canals and similar improvements, it will be productive of substantial utility. But there is reason to doubt, whether, in such channels, it is likely to find sufficient employment; and still more, whether many of those who possess it would be as readily attracted to objects of this nature, as to manufacturing pursuits, which bear greater analogy to those to which they are accustomed, and to the spirit generated by them.

To open the one field, as well as the other, will at least secure a better prospect of useful employment for whatever accession of money there has been or may be.

There is, at the present juncture, a certain fermentation of mind, a certain activity of speculation and enterprise, which, if properly directed, may be made subservient to useful purposes; but, which, if left entirely to itself, may be attended with pernicious effects.

The disturbed state of Europe inclining its citizens to emigration, the requisite workmen will be more easily acquired than at another time; and the effect of multiplying the opportunities of employment to those who emigrate, may be an increase of the number and extent of valuable acquisitions to the population, arts, and industry of the country.

To find pleasure in the calamities of other nations would be criminal; but to benefit ourselves by opening an asylum to those who suffer in consequence of them is as justifiable as it is politic.

A full view having now been taken of the inducements to the promotion of manufactures in the United States, accompanied with an examination of the principal objections which are commonly urged in opposition, it is proper, in the next place, to consider the means by which it may be affected, as introductory to a specification of the objects, which in the present state of things, appear the most fit to be encouraged, and of the particular measures which it may be advisable to adopt in respect to each.

In order to a better judgment of the means proper to be resorted to by the United States, it will be of use to advert to those which have been employed with success in other countries. The principal of these are:

1. Protecting duties — or duties on those foreign articles which are the rivals of the domestic ones intended to be encouraged.

Duties of this nature evidently amount to a virtual bounty on the domestic fabrics; since, by enhancing the charges on foreign fabrics, they enable the national manufacturers to undersell all their foreign competitors. The propriety of this species of encouragement need not be dwelt upon, as it is not only a clear result from the numerous topics which have been suggested, but is sanctioned by the laws of the United States, in a variety of instances; it has the additional recommendation of being a resource of revenue. Indeed, all the duties imposed on imported articles, though with an exclusive view to revenue, have the effect, in contemplation, and, except where they fall on raw materials, wear a beneficent aspect toward the manufactures of the country.

2. Prohibitions of rival articles, or duties equivalent to prohibitions.

This is another and efficacious means of encouraging national manufactures; but, in general, it is only fit to be employed when a manufacture has made such progress, and is in so many hands, as to insure a due competition, and an adequate supply on reasonable terms. Of duties equivalent to prohibitions, there are examples in the laws of the United States; and there are other cases to which the principle may be advantageously extended, but they are not numerous.

Considering a monopoly of the domestic market to its own manufactures as the reigning policy of manufacturing nations, a similar policy, on the part of the United States, in every proper instance, is dictated, it might almost be said, by the principles of distributive justice; certainly, by the duty of endeavoring to secure to their own citizens a reciprocity of advantages.

3. Prohibitions of the exportation of the materials of manufactures.

The desire of securing a cheap and plentiful supply for the national workmen, and where the article is either peculiar to the country or of peculiar quality there, the jealousy of enabling foreign workmen to rival those of the nation with its own materials, are the leading motives to this species of regulation. It ought not to be affirmed that it is in no instance proper; but it is, certainly, one which ought to be adopted with great circumspection, and only in very plain cases. It is seen at once, that its immediate operation is to abridge the demand, and keep down the price of the produce of some other branch of industry—generally speaking, of agriculture—to the prejudice of those who carry it on; and though, if it be really essential to the prosperity of any very important national manufacture, it may happen that those who are injured, in the first instance, may be, eventually, indemnified by the superior steadiness of an extensive domestic market, depending on that prosperity; yet, in a matter in which there is so much room for nice and difficult combinations, in which such opposite considerations combat each other, prudence seems to dictate that the expedient in question ought to be indulged with a sparing hand.

4. Pecuniary Bounties.

This has been found one of the most efficacious means of encouraging manufactures, and is, in some views, the best. Though it has not yet been practised upon by the government of the United States (unless the allowance on the exportation of dried and pickled fish and salted meat could be considered as a bounty), and though it is less favored by public opinion than some other modes, its advantages are these:

1. It is a species of encouragement more positive and direct than any other, and, for that very reason, has a more immediate tendency to stimulate and uphold new enterprises, increasing the chances of profit, and diminishing the risk of loss, in the first attempts.

2. It avoids the inconvenience of a temporary augmentation of price, which is incident to some other modes; or it produces it to a less degree, either by making no addition to the charges on the rival foreign article, as in the case of protecting duties, or by making a smaller addition. The first happens when the fund for the bounty is derived from a different object (which may or may not increase the price of some other article, according to the nature of that object; the second, when the fund is derived from the same or a similar object, of foreign manufacture. One per cent duty on the foreign article, converted into a bounty on the domestic, will have an equal effect with a duty of two per cent, exclusive of such bounty; and the price of the foreign commodity is liable to be raised, in the one case, in the proportion of one per cent; in the other, in that of two per cent. Indeed, the bounty when drawn from another source, is calculated to promote a reduction of price; because, without laying any new charge on the foreign article, it serves to introduce a competition with it, and to increase the total quantity of the article in the market.

3. Bounties have not, like high protecting duties, a tendency to produce scarcity. An increase of price is not always the immediate, though, where the progress of a domestic manufacture does not counteract a rise, it is, commonly, the ultimate effect of an additional duty. In the interval between the laying of the duty and the proportional increase of price, it may discourage importation, by interfering with the profits to be expected from the sale of the article.

4. Bounties are, sometimes, not only the best, but the only proper expedient for uniting the encouragement of a new object of agriculture with that of a new object of manufacture. It is the interest of the farmer to have the production of the raw material promoted by counteracting the interference of the foreign material of the same kind. It is the interest of the manufacturer to have the material abundant and cheap. If, prior to the domestic production of the material, in sufficient quantity to supply the manufacturer on good terms, a duty be laid upon the importation of it from abroad, with a view to promote the raising of it at home, the interest both of the farmer and manufacturer will be deserved. By either destroying the requisite supply, or raising the price of the article beyond what can be afforded to be given for it by the conductor of an infant manufacture, it is abandoned or fails, and there being no domestic manufactories to create a demand for the raw material, which is raised by the farmer, it is in vain that the competition of the like foreign article may have been destroyed.

It cannot escape notice, that a duty upon the importation of an article can no otherwise aid the domestic production of it, than by giving the latter greater advantages in the home market. It can have no influence upon the advantageous sale of the article produced in foreign markets — no tendency, therefore, to promote its exportation.

The true way to conciliate these two interests is to lay a duty on foreign manufactures of the material, the growth of which is desired to be encouraged, and to apply the produce of that duty, by way of bounty either upon the production of the material itself, or upon its manufacture at home, or upon both. In this disposition of the thing, the manufacturer commences his enterprise under every advantage which is attainable, as to quantity or price of the raw material; and the farmer, if the bounty be immediately to him, is enabled by it to enter into a successful competition with the foreign material. If the bounty be to the manufacturer, on so much of the domestic material as he consumes, the operation is nearly the same: he has a motive of interest to prefer the domestic commodity, if of equal quality, even at a higher price than the foreign, so long as the difference of price is anything short of the bounty which is allowed upon the article.

Except the simple and ordinary kinds of household manufacture, or those for which there are very commanding local advantages, pecuniary bounties are, in most cases, indispensable to the introduction of a new branch. A stimulus and a support, not less powerful and direct, is, generally speaking, essential to the overcoming of the obstacles which arise from the competitions of superior skill and maturity elsewhere. Bounties are especially essential in regard to articles upon which those foreigners, who have been accustomed to supply a country, are in the practice of granting them.

The continuance of bounties on manufactures long established must almost always be of questionable policy; because a presumption would arise, in every such case, that there were natural and inherent impediments to success. But, in new undertakings, they are as justifiable as they are oftentimes necessary.

There is a degree of prejudice against bounties, from an appearance of giving away the public money without an immediate consideration, and from a supposition that they serve to enrich particular classes at the expense of the community.

But neither of these sources of dislike will bear a serious examination. There is no purpose to which public money can be more beneficially applied than to the acquisition of a new and useful branch of industry; no consideration more valuable than a permanent addition to the general stock of productive labor.

As to the second source of objection, it equally lies against other modes of encouragement, which are admitted to be eligible. As often as a duty upon a foreign article makes an addition to its price, it causes an extra expense to the community for the benefit of the domestic manufacturer. A bounty does no more. But it is the interest of the society, in each case, to submit to the temporary expense — which is more than compensated by an increase of industry and wealth, by an augmentation of resources and independence, and by the circumstance of eventual cheapness, which has been noticed in another place.

It would deserve attention, however, in the employment of this species of encouragement in the United States, as a reason for moderating the degree of it in the instances in which it might be deemed eligible, that the great distance of this country from Europe imposes very heavy charges on all the fabrics which are brought from thence, amounting to from 15 to 30 per cent, on their value, according to their bulk.

A question has been made concerning the constitutional right of the Government of the United States to apply this species of encouragement, but there is certainly no good foundation for such a question. The National Legislature has express authority "to lay and collect taxes, duties, imposts, and excises, to pay the debts and provide for the common defence and general welfare," with no other qualifications than that "all duties, imposts, and excises shall be uniform throughout the United States; and that no capitation or other direct tax shall be laid, unless in proportion to numbers ascertained by a census or enumeration, taken on the principles prescribed in the Constitution," and that "no tax or duty shall be laid on articles exported from any State."

These three qualifications excepted, the power to raise money is plenary aud indefinite, and the objects to which it may be appropriated are no less comprehensive than the payment of the public debts, and the providing for the common defence and general welfare. The terms "general welfare" were doubtless intended to signify more than was expressed or imported in those which preceded; otherwise, numerous exigencies incident to the affairs of a nation would have been left without a provision. The phrase is as comprehensive as any that could have been used, because it was not fit that the constitutional authority of the Union to appropriate its revenues should have been restricted within narrower limits than the "general welfare," and because this necessarily embraces a vast variety of particulars, which are susceptible neither of specification nor of definition.

It is, therefore, of necessity, left to the discretion of the National Legislature to pronounce upon the objects which concern the general welfare, and for which, under that description, an appropriation of money is requisite and proper. And there seems to be no room for a doubt that whatever concerns the general interests of learning, of agriculture, of manufactures, and of commerce, are within the sphere of the national councils, as far as regards an application of money.

The only qualification of the generality of the phrase in question which seems to be admissable, is this: That the object to which an appropriation of money is to be made be general, and not local; its operation extending in fact or by possibility throughout the Union, and not being confined to a particular spot.

No objection ought to arise to this construction, from a supposition that it would imply a power to do whatever else should appear to Congress conducive to the general welfare. A power to appropriate money with this latitude, which is granted, too, in express terms, would not carry a power to do any other thing not authorized in the Constitution, either expressly or by fair implication.

5. *Premiums.* These are of nature allied to bounties, though distinguishable from them in some important features.

Bounties are applicable to the whole quantity of an article produced, or manufactured, or exported, and involve a correspondent expense. Premiums serve to reward some particular excellence or superiority, some extraordinary exertion of skill, and are dispensed only in a small number of cases. But their effect is to stimulate general effort; contrived so as to be both honorary and lucrative, they address themselves to different passions—touching the chords, as well of emulation as of interest. They are, accordingly, a very economical means of exciting the enterprise of a whole community.

There are various societies in different countries, whose object is the dispensation of premiums for the encouragement of agriculture, art, manufactures, and commerce; and though they are, for the most part, voluntary associations, with comparatively slender funds, their utility has been immense. Much has been done, by this means, in Great Britian. Scotland, in particular, owes materially to it a prodigious amelioration of condition. From a similiar establishment in the United States, supplied and supported by the Government of the Union, vast benefits might reasonably be expected. Some further ideas on this head shall, accordingly, be submitted in the conclusion of this report.

6. *The exemption of the materials of manufactures from duty.*

The policy of that exemption, as a general rule, particularly in reference to new establishments, is obvious. It can hardly ever be advisable to add the obstructions of fiscal burthens to the difficulties which naturally embarrass a new manufacture; and where it is matured, and in condition to become an object of revenue, it is, generally speaking, better that the fabric, than the material, should be the subject of taxation. Ideas of proportion between the quantum of the tax and the value of the article can be more easily adjusted in the former than in the latter case. An argument for exemptions of this kind, in the United States, is to be derived from the practice, as far as their necessities have permitted, of those nations whom we are to meet as competitors in our own and in foreign markets.

There are, however, exceptions to it, of which some examples will be given under the next head.

The laws of the Union afford instances of the observance of the policy here recommended, but it will probably be found advisable to extend it to some other cases. Of a nature bearing some affinity to that policy is the regulation, which exempts from duty the tools and implements, as well as the books, clothes, and household furniture, of foreign artists who come to reside in the United States—an advantage already secured to them by the laws of the Union, and which it is, in every view, proper to continue.

7. *Drawbacks of the duties which are imposed on the materials of manufactures.*

It has already been observed, as a general rule, that duties on those materials ought, with certain exceptions, to be forborne. Of these exceptions, three cases occur, which may serve as examples. One, where the material is itself an object of general or extensive consumption, and a fit and productive source of revenue. Another, where a manufacture of a simpler kind, the competition of which, with a like domestic article, is desired to be restrained, partakes of the nature of a raw material, from being capable, by a further process, to be converted into a manufacture of a different kind, the introduction or growth of which is desired to be encouraged. A third, where the material itself is a production of the country, and in sufficient abundance to furnish a cheap and plentiful supply to the national manufacturers.

Under the first description comes the article of molasses. It is not only a fair object of revenue, but, being a sweet, it is just that the consumers of it should pay a duty as well as the consumers of sugar.

Cottons and linens, in their white state, fall under the second description. A duty upon such as are imported is proper to promote the domestic manufacture of similar articles in the same State. A drawback of that duty is proper, to encourage the printing and staining at home of those which are brought from abroad. When the first of these manufactures has attained sufficient maturity in a country to furnish a full supply for the second, the utility of the drawback ceases.

The article of hemp either now does, or may be expected soon to, exemplify the third case in the United States.

Where duties on the materials of manufactures are not laid for the purpose of preventing a competition with some domestic production, the same reasons which recommend, as a general rule, the exemption of those materials from duties, would recommend, as a like general rule, the allowance of drawbacks in favor of the manufacturer. Accordingly, such drawbacks are familiar in countries which systematically pursue the business of manufactures; which furnishes an argument for the observance of a similar policy in the United States; and the idea has been adopted by the laws of the Union, in the instances of salt and molasses. It is believed that it will be found advantageous to extend it to some other articles.

8. The encouragement of new inventions and discoveries at home, and of the introduction into the United States of such as may have been made in other countries; particularly those which relate to machinery.

This is among the most useful and unexceptionable of the aids which can be given to manufactures. The usual means of that encouragement are pecuniary rewards, and, for a time, exclusive privileges. The first must be employed according to the occasion and the utility of the invention or discovery. For the last, so far as respects "authors and inventors," provision has been made by law. But it is desirable, in regard to improvements, and secrets of extraordinary value, to be able to extend the same benefit to introducers, as well as authors and inventors; a policy which has been practised with advantage in other countries. Here, however, as in some other cases, there is cause to regret that the competency of the authority of the National Government to the good which might be done, is not without a question. Many aids might be given to industry, many internal improvements of primary magnitude might be promoted, by an authority operating throughout the Union, which cannot be effected as well, if at all, by an authority confined within the limits of a single State.

But, if the legislature of the Union cannot do all the good that might be wished, it is, at least, desirable that all may be done which is practicable. Means for promoting the introduction of foreign improvements, though less efficaciously than might be accomplished with more adequate authority, will form a part of the plan intended to be submitted in the close of this report.

It is customary with manufacturing nations to prohibit, under severe penalties, the exportation of implements and machines which they have either invented or improved. There are already objects for a similar regulation in the United States; and others may be expected to occur from time to time. The adoption of it seems to be dictated by the principle of reciprocity. Greater liberality in such respects, might better comport with the general spirit of the country; but a selfish and exclusive policy, in other quarters, will not always permit the free indulgence of a spirit which would place us upon an unequal footing. As far as prohibitions tend to prevent foreign competitors from deriving the benefit of the improvements made at home, they tend to increase the advantages of those by whom they may have been introduced, and operate as an encouragement to exertion.

9. *Judicious regulations for the inspection of manufactured commodities.*

This is not among the least important of the means by which the prosperity of manufactures may be promoted. It is, indeed, in many cases, one of the most essential. Contributing to prevent frauds upon consumers at home and exporters to foreign countries, to improve the quality and preserve the character of the national manufactures, it cannot fail to aid the expeditious and advantageous sale of them, and to serve as a guard against successful competition from other quarters. The reputation of the flour and lumber of some States, and of the potash of others, has been established by an attention to this point. And the like good name might be procured for those articles, wheresoever produced, by a judicious and uniform system of inspection throughout the ports of the United States. A like system might also be extended with advantage to other commodities.

10. *The facilitating of pecuniary remittances from place to place—*

Is a point of considerable moment to trade in general, and to manufacturers in particular, by rendering more easy the purchase of raw materials and provisions, and the payment for manufactured supplies. A general circulation of bank paper, which is to be expected from the institution lately established, will be a most valuable means to this end. But much good would also accrue from some additional provisions respecting inland bills of exchange. If those drawn in one State, payable in another, were made negotiable everywhere, and interest and damages allowed in case of protest, it would greatly promote negotiations between the citizens of different States, by rendering them more secure, and with it the convenience and advantage of the merchants and manufacturers of each.

11. *The facilitating of the transportation of commodities.*

Improvements favoring this object intimately concern all the domestic interests of a community; but they may, without impropriety, be mentioned as having an important relation to manufacturers. There is, perhaps, scarcely anything which has been better calculated to assist the manufacturers of Great Britain, than the melioration of the public roads of that kingdom, and the great progress which has been of late made in opening canals. Of the former, the United States stand much in need; for the latter, they present uncommon facilities.

The symptoms of attention to the improvement of inland navigation, which have lately appeared in some quarters, must fill with pleasure every breast warmed with a true zeal for the prosperity of the country. These examples, it is to be hoped, will stimulate the exertions of the government and citizens of every State. There can certainly be no object more worthy of the cares of the local administrations; and it were to be wished that there was no doubt of the power of the National Government to lend its direct aid on a comprehensive plan. This is one of those improvements which could be prosecuted with more efficacy by the whole than by any part or parts of the Union. There are cases in which the general interest will be in danger to be sacrificed to the collision of some supposed local interests. Jealousies, in matters of this kind, are as apt to exist as they are apt to be erroneous.

The following remarks are sufficiently judicious and pertinent to deserve a literary quotation:

"Good roads, canals, and navigable rivers, by diminishing the expense of carriage, put the remote parts of a country more nearly upon a level with those in the neighborhood of the town. They are, upon that account, the greatest of all improvements. They encourage the cultivation of the remote, which must always be the most extensive circle of the country. They are advantageous to the town, by breaking down the monopoly of the country in its neighborhood. They are advantageous even to that part of the country. Though they introduce some rival commodities into the old market, they open many new markets to its produce. Monopoly, besides, is a great enemy to good management, which can never be universally established, but in consequence of that free and universal competition, which forces everybody to have recourse to it for the sake of self-defence. It is not more than fifty years ago that some of the counties in the neighborhood of London petitioned the Parliament against the extension of the turnpike roads into the remoter countries. Those remoter counties, they pretended, from the cheapness of labor, would be able to sell their grass and corn cheaper in the London market than themselves, and they would thereby reduce their rents and ruin their cultivation. Their rents, however, have risen, and their cultivation has improved since that time."

Specimens of a spirit similar to that which governed the counties here spoken of, present themselves too frequently to the eye of an impartial observer, and render it a wish of patriotism, that the body in this country, in whose councils a local or partial spirit is least likely to predominate, were at liberty to pursue and promote the general interest, in those instances in which there might be danger of the interference of such a spirit.

The foregoing are the principal of the means by which the growth of manufactures is ordinarily promoted. It is, however, not merely necessary that the measures of government which have a direct view to manufactures, should be calculated to assist and protect them, but that those which only collaterally effect them in the general course of the administration should be guarded from any peculiar tendency to injure them.

There are certain species of taxes, which are apt to be oppressive to different parts of the community, and, among other ill effects, have a very unfriendly aspect toward manufactures. All poll or capitation taxes are of this nature. They either proceed according to a fixed rate, which operates unequally and injuriously to the industrious poor, or they vest a discretion, in certain officers, to make estimates and assessments, which are necessarily vague, conjectural, and liable to abuse. They ought, therefore, to be abstained from in all but cases of distressing emergency.

All such taxes (including all taxes on occupations) which proceed according to the amount of capital supposed to be employed in a business, or of profits supposed to be made in it, are unavoidably hurtful to industry. It is in vain that the evil may be endeavored to be mitigated, by leaving it, in the first instance, in the option of the party to be taxed, to declare the amount of his capital or profits.

Men engaged in any trade or business have commonly weighty reasons to avoid disclosures which would expose, with anything like accuracy, the real state of their affairs. They most frequently find it better to risk oppression, than to avail themselves of so inconvenient a refuge, and the consequence is, that they often suffer oppression.

When the disclosure, too, if made, is not definite, but controllable by the discretion, or, in other words, by the passions and prejudices, of the revenue officers, it is not only an ineffectual protection, but the possibility of its being so is an additional reason for not resorting to it.

Allowing to the public officers the most equitable dispositions, yet, where they are to exercise a discretion without certain data, they cannot fail to be often misled by appearances. The quantity of business which seems to be going on is, in a vast number of cases, a very deceitful criterion of the profits which are made; yet it is, perhaps, the best they can have, and it is the one on which they will most naturally rely. A business, therefore, which may rather require aid from the government, than be in a capacity to be contributory to it, may find itself crushed by the mistaken conjectures of the assessors of taxes.

Arbitrary taxes, under which denomination are comprised all those that leave the quantum of the tax to be raised on each person to the discretion of certain officers, are as contrary to the genius of liberty as to the maxims of industry. In this light they have been viewed by the most judicious observers on government, who have bestowed upon them the severest epithets of reprobation, as constituting one of the worst features usually to be met with in the practice of despotic governments.

It is certain, at least, that such taxes are particularly inimical to the success of manufacturing industry, and ought carefully to be avoided by a government which desires to promote it.

The great copiousness of the subject of this report has insensibly led to a more lengthy preliminary discussion than was originally contemplated or intended. It appeared proper to investigate principles, to consider objections, and to endeavor to establish the utility of the thing proposed to be encouraged, previous to a specification of the objects which might occur, as meriting or requiring encouragement, and of the measures which might be proper in respect to each. The first purpose having been fulfilled, it remains to pursue the second.

In the selection of objects, five circumstances seem entitled to particular attention; the capacity of the country to furnish the raw material; the degree in which the nature of the manufacture admits of a substitute for manual labor in machinery; the facility of execution; the extensiveness of the uses to which the article can be applied; its subserviency to other interests, particularly the great one of national defence. There are, however, objects to which these circumstances are little applicable, which, for some special reasons, may have a claim to encouragement.

A designation of the principal raw material of which each manufacture is composed, will serve to introduce the remarks upon it; as, in the first place,

IRON.

The manufactures of this article are entitled to pre-eminent rank. None are more essential in their kinds, nor so extensive in their use. They constitute, in whole or in part, the implements or the materials, or both, of almost every useful occupation. Their instrumentality is everywhere conspicuous.

It is fortunate for the United States that they have peculiar advantages for deriving the full benefit of this most valuable material, and they have every motive to improve it with systematic care. It is to be found in various parts of the United States, in great abundance, and of almost every quality; and fuel, the chief instrument in manufacturing it, is both cheap and plenty. This particularly applies to charcoal; but there are productive coal mines already in operation, and strong indications that the material is to be found in abundance in a variety of other places.

The inquiries to which the subject of this report has led have been answered with proofs that manufactories of iron, though generally understood to be extensive, are far more so than is commonly supposed. The kinds in which the greatest progress has been made have been mentioned in another place, and need not be repeated; but there is little doubt that every other kind, with due cultivation, will rapidly succeed. It is worthy of remark that several of the particular trades of which it is the basis are capable of being carried on without the aid of large capitals.

Iron works have greatly increased in the United States, and are prosecuted with much more advantage than formerly. The average price, before the Revolution, was about sixty-four dollars per ton; at present, it is about eighty—a rise which is chiefly to be attributed to the increase of manufactures of the material.

The still further extension and multiplication of such manufactures will have the double effect of promoting the extraction of the metal itself, and of converting it to a greater number of profitable purposes.

Those manufactures, too, unite, in a greater degree than almost any others, the several requisites which have been mentioned as proper to be consulted in the selection of objects.

The only further encouragement of manufactories of this article, the propriety of which may be considered as unquestionable, seems to be an increase of the duties on foreign rival commodities.

Steel is a branch which has already made considerable progress, and it is ascertained that some new enterprises, on a more extensive scale, have been lately set on foot. The facility of carrying it to an extent which will supply all internal demands, and furnish a considerable surplus for exportation, cannot be doubted. The duty upon the importation of this article, which is, at present, seventy-five cents per cwt., may, it is conceived, be safely and advantageously extended to one hundred cents. It is desirable, by decisive arrangements, to second the efforts which are making in so very valuable a branch.

The United States, already, in a great measure, supply themselves with nails and spikes. They are able, and ought certainly, to do it entirely. The first and most laborious operation, in this manufacture, is performed by water mills; and of the persons afterwards employed, a great proportion are boys, whose early habits of industry are of importance to the community, to the present support of their families, and to their own future comfort. It is not less curious than true, that, in certain parts of the country, the making of nails is an occasional family manufacture.

The expediency of an additional duty on these articles is indicated by an important fact. About one million eight hundred thousand pounds of them were imported into the United States in the course of a year, ending the 30th of September, 1790. A duty of two cents a pound would, it is presumable, speedily put an end to so considerable an importation. And it is, in every view, proper that an end should be put to it.

The manufacture of these articles, like that of some others, suffers from the carelessness and dishonesty of a part of those who carry it on. An inspection in certain cases might tend to correct the evil. It will deserve consideration whether a regulation of this sort cannot be applied, without inconvenience, to the exportation of the articles, either to foreign countries, or from one State to another.

The implements of husbandry are made in several States in great abundance. In many places it is done by the common blacksmiths. And there is no doubt that an ample supply for the whole country can, with great ease, be procured among ourselves.

Various kinds of edged tools for the use of mechanics are also made; and a considerable quantity of hollow wares, though the business of castings has not yet attained the perfection which might be wished. It is, however, improving, and as there are respectable capitals, in good hands, embarked in the prosecution of those branches of iron manufacture which are yet in their infancy, they may all be contemplated as objects not difficult to be acquired.

To insure the end it seems equally safe and prudent to extend the duty, ad valorem, upon all manufactures of iron, or of which iron is the article of chief value, to ten per cent.

Fire-arms and other military weapons may, it is conceived, be placed, without inconvenience, in the class of articles rated at fifteen per cent. There are already manufactories of these articles, which only require the stimulus of a certain demand to render them adequate to the supply of the United States.

It would also be a material aid to manufactures of this nature, as well as a means of public security, if provision should be made for an annual purchase of military weapons, of home manufacture, to a certain determinate extent, in order to the formation of arsenals; and to replace, from time to time, such as should be drawn for use, so as to always have in store the quantity of each kind which should be deemed a competent supply.

But it may, hereafter, deserve legislative consideration, whether manufactories of all the necessary weapons of war ought not to be established on account of the government itself. Such establishments are agreeable to the usual practice of nations, and that practice seems founded on sufficient reason.

There appears to be an improvidence in leaving these essential implements of national defence to the casual speculations of individual adventure—a resource which can less be relied upon, in this case, than in most others; the articles in question not being objects of ordinary and indispensable private consumption or use. As a general rule, manufactories on the immediate account of government are to be avoided; but this seems to be one of the few exceptions which that rule admits, depending on very special reasons.

Manufacturers of steel, generally, or of which steel is the article of chief value, may, with advantage, be placed in the class of goods rated at seven and a half per cent. As manufactures of this kind have not yet made any considerable progress, it is a reason for not rating them as high as those of iron; but as this material is the basis of them, and as their extension is not less practicable than important, it is desirable to promote it by a somewhat higher duty than the present.

A question arises how far it might be expedient to permit the importation of iron, in pigs and bars, free from duty. It would certainly be favorable to manufactures of the article; but the doubt is, whether it might not interfere with its production.

Two circumstances, however, abate, if they do not remove, apprehension on this score; one is the considerable increase of price which has been already remarked, and which renders it probable that the free admission of foreign iron would not be inconsistent with an adequate profit to the proprietors of iron works; the other is the augmentation of demand which would be likely to attend the increase of manufactures of the article, in consequence of the additional encouragements proposed to be given. But caution, nevertheless, in a matter of this kind is most advisable. The measure suggested ought, perhaps, rather to be contemplated subject to the lights of further experience, than immediately adopted.

COPPER.

The manufactures of which this article is susceptible are, also, of great extent and utility. Under this description, those of brass, of which it is the principal ingredient, are intended to be included.

The material is a natural production of the country. Mines of copper have actually been wrought, and with profit to the undertakers, though it is not known that any are now in this condition. And nothing is easier than the introduction of it from other countries, on moderate terms and in great plenty.

Coppersmiths and brass founders, particularly the former, are numerous in the United States; some of whom carry on business to a respectable extent.

To multiply and extend manufactories of the materials in question, is worthy of attention and effort. In order to this, it is desirable to facilitate a plentiful supply of the materials; and a proper means to this end is to place them in the class of free articles. Copper, in plates, and brass, are already in this predicament; but copper, in pigs and bars, is not; neither is lapis calaminaris; which, together with copper and charcoal, constitute the component ingredients of brass. The exemption from duty, by parity of reason, ought to embrace all such of these articles as are objects of importation.

An additional duty on brass wares will tend to the general end in view. These now stand at five per cent, while those of tin, pewter, and copper are rated at seven and a half. There appears to be a propriety, in every view, in placing brass wares on the same level with them; and it merits consideration, whether the duty upon all of them ought not to be raised to ten per cent.

LEAD.

There are numerous proofs that this material abounds in the United States, and requires little to unfold it to an extent more than equal to every domestic occasion. A prolific mine of it has long been open in the southwestern parts of Virginia, and under a public administration during the late war, yielded a considerable supply for military use. This is now in the hands of individuals, who not only carry it on with spirit, but have established manufactories of it at Richmond, in the same State.

The duties already laid upon the importation of this article, either in its unmanufactured or manufactured state, insure it a decisive advantage in the home market, which amounts to considerable encouragement. If the duty on pewter wares should be raised, it would afford a further encouragement. Nothing else occurs as proper to be added.

FOSSIL COAL.

This, as an important instrument of manufactures, may, without impropriety, be mentioned among the subjects of this report.

A copious supply of it would be of great consequence to the iron branch. As an article of household fuel, also, it is an interesting production, the utility of which must increase in proportion to the decrease of wood, by the progress of settlement and cultivation. And its importance to navigation, as an immense article of transportation coastwise, is signally exemplified in Great Britain.

It is known that there are several coal mines in Virginia now worked; and appearances of their existence are familiar in a number of places.

The expediency of a bounty on all this species of coal, of home production, and of premiums on the opening of new mines, under certain qualifications, appears to be worthy of particular examination. The great importance of the article will amply justify a reasonable expense in this way, if it shall appear to be necessary to, and shall be thought likely to, answer the end.

WOOD.

Several manufactures of this article flourish in the United States. Ships are nowhere built in greater perfection, and cabinet wares generally are made little, if at all, inferior to those of Europe. Their extent is such as to have admitted of considerable exportation.

An exemption from duty of the several kinds of wood, ordinarily used in these manufactures, seems to be all that is requisite by way of encouragement. It is recommended by the consideration of a similar policy being pursued in other countries, and by the expediency of giving equal advantages to our own workmen in wood. The abundance of timber proper for ship-building in the United States does not appear to be any objection to it. The increasing scarcity and growing importance of that article, in the European countries, admonish the United States to commence, and systematically to pursue, measures for the preservation of their stock. Whatever may promote the regular establishment of magazines of ship timber is in various views desirable.

SKINS.

There are scarcely any manufactories of greater importance than of this article. Their direct and very happy influence upon agriculture, by promoting the raising of cattle of different kinds, is a very material recommendation.

It is pleasing, too, to observe the extensive progress they have made in their principal branches, which are so far matured as almost to defy foreign competition. Tanneries, in particular, are not only carried on as a regular business, in numerous instances, and in various parts of the country, but they constitute, in some places, a valuable item of incidental family manufactures.

Representations, however, have been made, importing the expediency of further encouragement to the leather branch, in two ways: one by increasing the duty on the manufactures of it which are imported; the other, by prohibiting the exportation of bark. In support of the latter, it is alleged, that the price of bark, chiefly in consequence of large exportations, has risen, within a few years, from about three dollars to four and a half per cord.

These suggestions are submitted, rather as intimations which merit consideration, than as matters the propriety of which is manifest. It is not clear that an increase of duty is necessary; and in regard to the prohibitions desired, there is no evidence of any considerable exportation hitherto; and it is most probable, that whatever augmentation of price may have taken place, is to be attributed to an extension of the home demand, from the increase of manufactures, and to a decrease of the supply, in consequence of the progress of settlement, rather than to the quantities which have been exported.

It is mentioned, however, as an additional reason for the prohibition, that one species of the bark usually exported, is in some sort peculiar to the country, and the material of a very valuable dye, of great use in some other manufactures, in which the United States have begun a competition.

There may also be this argument in favor of an increase of duty. The object is of importance enough to claim decisive encouragement, and the progress which has been made leaves no room to apprehend any inconvenience on the score of supply, from such an increase.

It would be of benefit to this branch if glue, which is now rated at five per cent, were made the object of an excluding duty. It is already made, in large quantities, at various tanneries, and, like paper, is an entire economy of materials, which, if not manufactured, would be left to perish. It may be placed, with advantage, in the class of articles paying fifteen per cent.

GRAIN.

Manufactures of the several species of this article have a title to peculiar favor, not only because they are, most of them, immediately connected with the subsistence of the citizens, but because they enlarge the demand for the most precious products of the soil.

Though flour may with propriety be noticed as a manufacture

of grain, it were useless to do it, but for the purpose of submitting the expediency of a general system of inspection throughout the ports of the United States, which, if established upon proper principles, would be likely to improve the quality of our flour everywhere, and to raise its reputation in foreign markets. There are, however, considerations which stand in the way of such an arrangement.

Ardent spirits and malt liquors are, next to flour, the two principal manufactures of grain. The first has made a very extensive, the last a considerable progress in the United States. In respect to both an exclusive possession of the home market ought to be secured to the domestic manufacturers as fast as circumstances will admit. Nothing is more practicable, and nothing more desirable.

The existing laws of the United States have done much towards attaining this valuable object, but some additions to the present duties on foreign distilled spirits and foreign malt liquors, and perhaps an abatement of those on home-made spirits, would more effectually secure it, and there does not occur any very weighty objection to either.

An augmentation of the duties on imported spirits would favor as well the distillation of spirits from molasses as that from grain; and to secure to the nation the benefit of a manufacture, even of foreign materials, is always of great, though perhaps of secondary importance.

A strong impression prevails in the minds of those concerned in distilleries (including, too, the most candid and enlightened), that greater differences in the rates of duty on foreign and domestic spirits are necessary completely to secure the successful manufacture of the latter and there are facts which entitle this impression to attention.

It is known that the price of molasses for some years past has been successively rising in the West India markets, owing partly to a competition which did not formerly exist, and partly to an extension of demand in this country; and it is evident that the late disturbances in those islands, from which we draw our principal supply, must so far interfere with the production of the article as to occasion a material enhancement in price. The destruction and devastation attendant on the insurrection in Hispaniola, in particular, must not only contribute very much to that effect, but may be expected to give it some duration. These circumstances, and the duty of three cents per gallon on molasses, may render it difficult for the distillers of that material to maintain with adequate profit a competition with the rum brought from the West Indies, the quality of which is so considerably superior.

The consumption of geneva, or gin, in this country is extensive. It is not long since distilleries of it have grown up among us to any importance. They are now becoming of consequence, but being still in their infancy, they require protection.

It is represented that the price of some of the materials is greater here than in Holland, from which place large quantities are brought; the price of labor considerably greater; capitals engaged in the business there much larger than those which are employed here; the rate of profits at which the undertakers can afford to carry it on much less; the prejudices in favor of importing gin strong. These circumstances are alleged to outweigh the charges which attend the bringing of the article from Europe to the United States and the present difference of duty, so as to obstruct the prosecution of the manufacture with due advantage.

Experiment could, perhaps, alone decide with certainty the justness of the suggestions which are made; but in relation to branches of manufacture so important, it would seem inexpedient to hazard an unfavorable issue, and better to err on the side of too great than of too small a difference in the particular in question.

It is, therefore, submitted, that an addition of two cents per gallon be made to the duty on imported spirits of the first class of proof, with a proportionable increase on those of higher proof; and that a deduction of one cent per gallon be made from the duty on spirits distilled within the United States, beginning with the first class of proof and a proportionable deduction from the duty on those of higher proof.

It is ascertained that by far the greatest part of the malt liquors consumed in the United States are the produce of domestic breweries. It is desirable, and in all likelihood attainable, that the whole consumption should be supplied by ourselves.

The malt liquors at home, though inferior to the best, are equal to a great part of those which have been usually imported. The progress already made is an earnest of what may be accomplished. The growing competition is an assurance of improvement. This will be accelerated by measures tending to invite a greater capital into this channel of employment.

To render the encouragement of domestic breweries decisive, it may be advisable to substitute to the present rates of duty, eight cents per gallon, generally; and it will deserve to be considered as a guard against evasions, whether there ought not to be a prohibition of their importation, except in casks of considerable capacity. It is to be hoped, that such a duty would banish from the market foreign malt liquors of inferior quality, and that the best kind, only, would continue to be imported, till it should be supplanted by the efforts of equal skill or care at home.

Till that period, the importation, so qualified, would be a useful stimulus to improvement, and, in the meantime, the payment of the increased price for the enjoyment of a luxury, in order to the encouragement of a most useful branch of domestic industry, could not reasonably be deemed a hardship.

As a further aid to manufactures of grain, though upon a smaller scale, the articles of starch, hair powder, and wafers may with great propriety be placed among those which are rated at fifteen per cent. No manufactures are more simple, nor more completely within the reach of a full supply from domestic sources; and it is a policy as common as it is obvious, to make them the objects either of prohibitionary duties or of express prohibition.

FLAX AND HEMP.

Manufactures of these articles have so much affinity to each other and they are so often blended, that they may, with advantage, be considered in conjunction. The importance of the linen branch to agriculture, its precious effects upon household industry, the ease with which the materials can be produced at home, to any requisite extent, the great advances which have been already made in the coarser fabrics of them, especially in the family way, constitute claims of peculiar force to the patronage of government.

This patronage may be afforded in various ways; by promoting the growth of the materials, by increasing the impediments to an advantageous competition of rival foreign articles, by direct bounties, or premiums upon the home manufactures.

1st. As to promoting the growth of the materials.

In respect to hemp, something has been already done, by the high duty upon foreign hemp. If the facilities for domestic production were not unusually great, the policy of the duty on the foreign raw material would be highly questionable, as interfering with the growth or manufactures of it. But making the proper allowances for those facilities, and with an eye to the future and natural progress of the country, the measure does not appear, upon the whole, exceptionable.

A strong wish naturally suggests itself, that some method could be devised, of affording a more direct encouragement to the growth both of flax and hemp; such as would be effectual, and at the same time, not attended with too great inconveniences. To this end, bounties and premiums offer themselves to consideration, but no modification of them has yet occurred, which would not either hazard too much expense, or operate unequally, in reference to the circumstances of different parts of the Union; and which would not be attended with very great difficulties in the execution.

2d. As to increasing the impediments to an advantageous competition of rival foreign articles.

To this purpose an augmentation of the duties on importation is the obvious expedient, which, in regard to certain articles, appears to be recommended by sufficient reasons.

The principal of these articles is sail-cloth—one intimately connected with navigation and defence, and of which a flourishing manufactory is established at Boston, and very promising ones at several other places.

It is presumed to be both safe and advisable to place this in the class of articles rated at ten per cent. A strong reason for it results from the consideration that a bounty of two pence sterling, per ell, is allowed in great Britain upon the exportation of the sail-cloth manufactured in that kingdom.

It would likewise appear to be good policy to raise the duty to seven and a half per cent on the following articles: Drillings, osnaburgs, ticklenburgs, dowals, canvass, brown rolls, bagging, and upon all other linens, the first cost of which, at the place of exportation, does not exceed thirty-five cents per yard. A bounty of twelve and a half per cent, upon an average, on the exportation of such or similar linens from Great Britain, encourages the manufacture of them in that country, and increases the obstacles to a successful competition in the countries to which they are sent.

The quantities of tow and other household linens, manufactured in different parts of the United States, and the expectations which are derived from some late experiments, of being able to extend the use of labor-saving machines, in the coarser fabrics of linen obviate the danger of inconvenience from an increase of the duty upon such articles, and authorize a hope of speedy and complete success to the endeavors which may be used for procuring an internal supply.

3d. As to direct bounties or premiums upon the manufactured articles.

To afford more effectual encouragement to the manufacture, and at the same time to promote the cheapness of the article, for the benefit of navigation, it will be of great use to allow a bounty of two cents per yard on all sail-cloth which is made in the United States, from materials of their own growth. This would also assist the culture of those materials. An encouragement of this kind, if adopted, ought to be established for a moderate term of years, to invite to new undertakings, and to an extension of the old. This is an article of importance enough to warrant the employment of extraordinary means in its favor.

COTTON.

There is something in the texture of this material which adapts it, in a peculiar degree, to the application of machines. The signal utility of the mill for spinning of cotton, not long since invented in England, has been noticed in another place; but there are other machines scarcely inferior in utility, which, in the different manufactories of this article, are employed, either exclusively, or with more than ordinary effect. This very important circumstance recommends the fabrics of cotton, in a more particular manner, to a country in which a defect of hands constitutes the greatest obstacle to success.

The variety and extent of the uses to which the manufactures of this article are applicable is another powerful argument in their favor. And the faculty of the United States to produce the raw material in abundance and of a quality, which, though alleged to be inferior to some that is produced in other quarters, is nevertheless capable of being used with advantage in many fabrics, and is probably susceptible of being carried by a more experienced culture to much greater perfection, suggests an additional and a very cogent inducement to the vigorous pursuit of the cotton branch in its several subdivisions. How much has been already done has been stated in a preceding part of this report.

In addition to this, it may be announced, that a society is forming, with a capital which is expected to be extended to at least half a million of dollars, on behalf of which, measures are already in train for prosecuting, on a large scale, the making and printing of cotton goods.

These circumstances conspire to indicate the expediency of removing any obstructions which may happen to exist, to the advantageous prosecution of the manufactories in question, and of adding such encouragements as may appear necessary and proper.

The present duty of three cents per pound on the foreign raw material is undoubtedly a very serious impediment to the progress of those manufactories.

The injurious tendency of similar duties, either prior to the establishment or in the infancy of the domestic manufacture of the article, as it regards the manufacture, and their worse than inutility, in relation to the home production of the material itself, have been anticipated, particularly in discussing the subject of pecuniary bounties.

Cotton has not the same pretensions with hemp, to form an exception to the general rule.

Not being, like hemp, a universal production of the country, it affords less assurance of an adequate internal supply; but the chief objection arises from the doubts which are entertained, concerning the quality of the national cotton. It is alleged that the fibre of it is considerably shorter and weaker than that of some other places; and it has been observed, as a general rule, that the nearer the place of growth to the equator, the better the quality of the cotton. That which comes from Cayenne, Surinam, and Demarara, is said to be preferable, even at a material difference of price, to the cotton of the islands.

While a hope may reasonably be indulged, that with due care and attention, the national cotton may be made to approach nearer than it now does to that of regions somewhat more favored by climate; and while facts authorize an opinion that very great use may be made of it, and that it is a resource which gives greater security to the cotton fabrics of this country, than can be enjoyed by any which depends wholly on external supply, it will certainly be wise, in every view, to let our infant manufactures have the full benefit of the best materials, on the cheapest terms. It is obvious that the necessity of having such materials is proportioned to the unskilfulness and inexperience of the workmen employed, who, if inexpert, will not fail to commit great waste, where the materials they are to work with are of an indifferent kind.

To secure to the national manufactures so essential an advantage, a repeal of the present duty on imported cotton is indispensable.

A substitute for this, far more encouraging to domestie production, will be to grant a bounty on the national cotton, when wrought at a home manufactory; to which a bounty on the exportation of it may be added. Either, or both, would do much more towards promoting the growth of the article, than the merely nominal encouragement, which it is proposed to abolish. The first would also have a direct influence in encouraging the manufacture.

The bounty which has been mentioned, as existing in Great Britain, upon the exportation of coarse linens, not exceeding a certain value, applies also to certain descriptions of cotton goods of similar value.

This furnishes an additional argument for allowing to the national manufactures the species of encouragement just suggested, and, indeed, for adding some other aid.

One cent per yard, not less than of a given width, on all goods of cotton, or of cotton and linen mixed, which are manufactured in the United States, with the addition of one cent per pound weight of the material, if made of national cotton, would amount to an aid of considerable importance, both to the production and to the manufacture of that valuable article. And it is conceived that the expense would be well justified by the magnitude of the object.

The printing and staining of cotton goods is known to be a distinct business from the fabrication of them. It is one easily accomplished, and which, as it adds materially to the value of the article in its white state, and prepares it for a variety of new uses, is of importance to be promoted.

As imported cottons, equally with those which are made at home, may be the objects of this manufacture, it will merit consideration, whether the whole, or a part of the duty, on the white goods, ought not to be allowed to be drawn back in favor of those who print or stain them. This measure would certainly operate as a powerful encouragement to the business; and though it may, in a degree, counteract the original fabrication of the articles, it would probably more than compensate for this disadvantage, in the rapid growth of a collateral branch, which is of a nature sooner to attain to maturity. When a sufficient progress shall have been made, the drawback may be abrogated, and by that time the domestic supply of the articles to be printed or stained will have been extended.

If the duty of seven and a half per cent on certain kinds of cotton goods were extended to all goods of cotton, or of which it is the principal material, it would probably more than counterbalance the effect of the drawback proposed, in relation to the fabrication of the article. And no material objection occurs to such an extension. The duty, then, considering all the circumstances which attend goods of this description, could not be deemed inconveniently high; and it may be inferred, from various causes, that the prices of them would still continue moderate.

Manufactories of cotton goods, not long since established at Beverly, in Massachusetts, and at Providence, in the State of Rhode Island, and conducted with a perseverance corresponding with the patriotic motives which began them, seem to have overcome the first obstacles to success; producing corduroys, velverets, fustians, jeans, and other similar articles, of a quality which will bear a comparison with the like articles brought from Manchester. The one at Providence has the merit of being the first introducing into the United States the celebrated cotton mill, which not only furnishes materials for that manufactory itself but for the supply of private families, for household manufacture.

Other manufactories of the same material, as regular businesses, have also been begun at different places in the State of Connecticut, but all upon a smaller scale than those above mentioned. Some essays are also making in the printing and staining of cotton goods. There are several small establishments of this kind already on foot.

WOOL.

In a country, the climate of which partakes of so considerable a proportion of winter, as that of a great part of the United States, the woollen branch cannot be regarded as inferior to any, which relates to the clothing of the inhabitants.

Household manufactures of this material are carried on in different parts of the United States, to a very interesting extent; but there is only one branch, which, as a regular business, can be said to have acquired maturity. This is the making of hats.

Hats of wool and of wool mixed with fur are made in large quantities, in different States; and nothing seems wanting, but an adequate supply of materials, to render the manufacture commensurate with the demand.

A promising essay towards the fabrication of cloths, cassimeres, and other woollen goods, is likewise going on at Hartford, in Connecticut. Specimens of the different kinds which are made, in the possession of the Secretary, evince that these fabrics have attained a very considerable degree of perfection. Their quality certainly surpasses anything that could have been looked for in so short a time, and under so great disadvantages; and conspires, with the scantiness of the means, which have been at the command of the directors, to form the eulogium of that public spirit, perseverance and judgment, which have been able to accomplish so much.

To cherish and bring to maturity this precious embryo must engage the most ardent wishes and proportionable regret as far as the means of doing it may appear difficult or uncertain.

Measures, which should tend to promote an abundant supply of wool of good quality, would probably afford the most efficacious aid that present circumstances permit.

To encourage the raising and improving the breed of sheep at home would certainly be the most desirable expedient for that purpose; but it may not be alone sufficient, especially as it is, yet, a problem, whether our wool be capable of such a degree of improvement as to render it fit for the finer fabrics.

Premiums would probably be found the best means of promoting the domestic and bounties the foreign supply. The first may be within the compass of the institution, hereafter to be submitted. The last would require a specific legislative provision. If any bounties are granted, they ought, of course, to be adjusted with an eye to quality as well as quantity.

A fund for the purpose may be derived from the addition of two and a half per cent to the present rate of duty on carpets and carpeting; an increase to which the nature of the articles suggests no objection, and which may, at the same time furnish a motive the more to the fabrication of them at home, towards which some beginnings have been made.

SILK.

The production of this article is attended with great facility in most parts of the United States. Some pleasing essays are making in Connecticut, as well towards that, as towards the manufacture of what is produced. Stockings, handkerchiefs, ribbons, and buttons are made, though as yet but in small quantities.

A manufactory of lace, upon a scale not very extensive, has been long memorable at Ispwich, in the State of Massachusetts.

An exemption of the material from the duty which it now pays on importation, and premiums upon the production to be dispensed under the direction of the institution before alluded to, seem to be the only species of encouragement advisable at so early a stage of the thing.

GLASS.

The materials for making glass are found everywhere. In the United States there is no deficiency of them. The sands and stones called tarso, which include flinty and crystalline substances generally, and the salts of various plants, particularly of the sea-weed, kali or kelp, constitute the essential ingredients. An extraordinary abundance of fuel is a particular advantage enjoyed by this country for such manufactures. They, however, require large capitals, and involve much manual labor.

Different manufactories of glass are now on foot in the United States. The present duty of twelve and a half per cent on all imported articles of glass amounts to a considerable encouragement to those manufactories. If anything in addition is judged eligible, the most proper would appear to be a direct bounty on window glass and black bottles.

The first recommends itself as an object of general convenience; the last adds to that character the circumstance of being an important item in breweries. A complaint is made of great deficiency in this respect.

GUNPOWDER.

No small progress has been, of late, made in the manufacture of this very important article. It may, indeed, be considered as already established; but its high importance renders its further extension very desirable.

The encouragement which it already enjoys, are a duty of ten per cent on the foreign rival article, and an exemption of saltpetre, one of the principal ingredients of which it is composed, from duty. A like exemption of sulphur, another cheap ingredient, would appear to be equally proper. No quantity of this article has yet been produced from internal sources. The use made of it in finishing the bottoms of ships, is an additional inducement to placing it in the class of free goods. Regulations for the careful inspection of the article would have a favorable tendency.

PAPER.

Manufactories of paper are among those which are arrived at the greatest maturity in the United States, and are most adequate to national supply. That of paper-hangings, is a branch in which respectable progress has been made.

Nothing material seems wanting to the further success of this valuable branch, which is already protected by a competent duty on similar imported articles.

In the enumeration of the several kinds made subject to that duty, sheathing and cartridge paper have been omitted. These being the most simple manufactures of the sort, and necessary to military supply, as well as ship-building, recommend themselves equally with those of other descriptions, to encouragement, and appear to be as fully within the compass of domestic exertions.

PRINTED BOOKS.

The great number of presses disseminated throughout the Union, seem to afford an assuranee that there is no need of being indebted to foreign countries for the printing of the books which are used in the United States. A duty of ten per cent, instead of five, which is now charged upon the article, would have a tendency to aid the business internally.

It occurs as an objection to this, that it may have an unfavorable aspect toward literature, by raising the price of books in universal use in private families, schools, and other seminaries of learning. But the difference, it is conceived, would be without effect.

As to books which usually fill the libraries of the wealthier classes and of professional men, such an augmentation of price as might be occasioned by an additional duty of five per cent, would be too little felt to be an impediment to the acquisition.

And with regard to books which may be specially imported for the use of particular seminaries of learning and of public libraries, a total exemption from duty would be advisable, which would go far towards obviating the objection just mentioned. They are now subject to a duty of five per cent.

As to the books in most general family use, the constancy and universality of the demand would insure exertions to furnish them at home, and the means are completely adequate. It may also be expected ultimately, in this as in other cases, that the extension of the domestic manufacture would conduce to the cheapness of the article.

It ought not to pass unremarked, that to encourage the printing of books is to encourage the manufacture of paper.

REFINED SUGARS AND CHOCOLATE

Are among the number of extensive and prosperous domestic manufactures.

Drawbacks of the duties upon the materials of which they are respectively made, in cases of exportation, would have a beneficial influence upon the manufacture, and would conform to a precedent which has been already furnished in the instance of molasses, on the exportation of distilled spirits.

Cocoa, the raw material, now pays a duty of one cent per pound, while chocolate, which is a prevailing and very simple manufacture, is comprised in the mass of articles rated at no more than five per cent.

There would appear to be a propriety in encouraging the manufacture by a somewhat higher duty on its foreign rival, than is paid on the raw material. Two cents per pound on imported chocolate would, it is presumed, be without inconvenience.

The foregoing heads comprise the most important of the several kinds of manufactures which have occurred as requiring, and, at the same time, as most proper for public encouragement; and such measures for affording it as have appeared best calculated to answer the end, have been suggested.

The observations, which have accompanied this delineation of objects, supersede the necessity of many supplementary remarks. One or two, however, may not be altogether superfluous.

Bounties are in various instances proposed as one species of encouragement.

It is a familiar objection to them that they are difficult to be managed, and liable to frauds. But neither that difficulty nor this danger seems sufficiently great to countervail the advantages of which they are productive when rightly applied. And it is presumed to have been shown that they are, in some cases, particularly in the infancy of new enterprises, indispensable.

It will, however, be necessary to guard, with extraordinary circumspection, the manner of dispensing them. The requisite precautions have been thought of, but to enter into the detail would swell this report, already voluminous, to a size too inconvenient.

If the principle shall not be deemed inadmissible, the means of avoiding an abuse of it will not be likely to present insurmountable obstacles. There are useful guides from practice in other quarters.

It shall, therefore, only be remarked here, in relation to this point that any bounty which may be applied to the manufacture of an article, cannot, with safety, extend beyond those manufactories at which the making of the article is a regular trade. It would be impossible to annex adequate precautions to a benefit of that nature, if extended to every private family in which the manufacture was incidentally carried on; and, being a merely incidental occupation which engages a portion of time that would otherwise be lost, it can be advantageously carried on without so special an aid.

The possibility of a diminution of the revenue may also present itself as an objection to the arrangements which have been submitted.

But there is no truth which may be more firmly relied upon, than that the interests of the revenue are promoted by whatever promotes an increase of national industry and wealth.

In proportion to the degree of these, is the capacity of every country to contribute to the public treasure; and where the capacity to pay is increased, or even is not decreased, the only consequence of measures which diminish any particular resource, is a change of the object. If, by encouraging the manufacture of an article at home, the revenue which has been wont to accrue from its importation should be lessened, an indemnification can easily be found, either out of the manufacture itself, or from some other object which may be deemed more eonvenient.

The measures, however, which have been submitted, taken aggregately, will, for a long time to come, rather augment than decrease the public revenue.

There is little room to hope, that the progress of manufactures will so equally keep pace with the progress of population, as to prevent even a gradual augmentation of the product of the duties on imported articles.

As, nevertheless, an abolition in some instances, and a reduction in others, of duties which have been pledged for the public debt, is proposed, it is essential that it should be accompanied with a competent substitute. In order to this, it is requisite that all the additional duties which shall be laid, be appropriated, in the first instance, to replace all defalcations which may proceed from any such abolition or diminution. It is evident, at first glance, that they will not only be adequate to this, but will yield a considerable surplus. This surplus will serve:

First. To constitute a fund for paying the bounties which shall have been decreed.

Secondly. To constitute a fund for the operations of a board to to be established, for promoting arts, agriculture, manufactures, and commerce. Of this institution, different intimations have been given in the course of this report. An outline of a plan for it shall now be submitted.

Let a certain annual sum be set apart, and placed under the management of commissioners, not less than three, to consist of certain officers of the government and their successors in office.

Let these commissioners be empowered to apply the fund confided to them, to defray the expenses of the emigration of artists and manufacturers in particular branches of extraordinary importance; to induce the prosecution and introduction of useful discoveries, inventions, and improvements, by proportionate rewards, judiciously held out and applied; to encourage by premiums, both honorable and lucrative, the exertions of individuals and of classes, in relation to the several objects they are charged with promoting; and to afford such other aids to those objects as may be generally designated by law.

The commissioners to render to the Legislature an annual account of their transactions and disbursements; and all such sums as shall not have been applied to the purposes of their trust at the end of every three years, to revert to the treasury. It may, also, be enjoined upon them not to draw out the money, but for the purpose of some specific disbursement.

It may, moreover, be of use to authorize them to receive voluntary contributions, making it their duty to apply them to the particular objects for which they may have been made, if any shall have been designated by the donors.

There is reason to believe that the progress of particular manufactures has been much retarded by the want of skilful workmen. And it often happens, that the capitals employed are not equal to the purposes of bringing from abroad workmen of a superior kind. Here, in cases worthy of it, the auxiliary agency of government would, in all probability, be useful. There are also valuable workmen in every branch, who are prevented from emigrating, solely, by the want of means. Occasional aids to such persons, properly administered, might be a source of valuable acquisitions to the country.

The propriety of stimulating by rewards the invention and introduction of useful improvements, is admitted without difficulty. But the success of attempts in this way must evidently depend much on the manner of conducting them. It is probable that the placing of the dispensation of those rewards under some proper discretionary direction where they may be accompanied by collateral expedients, will serve to give them the surest efficacy. It seems impracticable to apportion, by general rules, specific compensations for discoveries of unknown and disproportionate utility.

The great use which may be made of a fund of this nature, to procure and import foreign improvements, is particularly obvious. Among these, the article of machines would form a most important item.

The operation and utility of premiums have been adverted to, together with the advantages which have resulted from their dispensation, under the direction of certain public and private societies. Of this, some experience has been had, in the instance of the Pennsylvania Society for the promotion of manufactures and useful arts; but the funds of that association have been too contracted to produce more than a very small portion of the good to which the principles of it would have led. It may confidently be affirmed, that there is scarcely anything which has been devised, better calculated to excite a general spirit of improvement than the institutions of this nature. They are truly invaluable.

In countries where there is great private wealth, much may be effected by the voluntary contributions of patriotic individuals, but in a community situated like that of the United States, the public purse must supply the deficiency of private resource. In what can it be so useful, as in prompting and improving the efforts of industry?

Spotted something that isn't quite right?

Let us know and we'll fix it for future reprints.
And as a thank you for your diligence, we'll
send you a free Sothis book of your choice.

publisher@sothis.press

This page intentionally left blank

Made in the USA
Las Vegas, NV
27 October 2026

56676793R00059